WE SURVIVED

ROBERT HARDGRAVE

Copyright © 2022 Robert Hardgrave.

All rights reserved. No part of this book may be reproduced, stored, or transmitted by any means—whether auditory, graphic, mechanical, or electronic—without written permission of both publisher and author, except in the case of brief excerpts used in critical articles and reviews. Unauthorized reproduction of any part of this work is illegal and is punishable by law.

ISBN: 978-1-956373-04-2 (sc)
ISBN: 978-1-949735-17-8 (hc)
ISBN: 978-1-956373-00-4 (e)

Because of the dynamic nature of the Internet, any web addresses or links contained in this book may have changed since publication and may no longer be valid. The views expressed in this work are solely those of the author and do not necessarily reflect the views of the publisher, and the publisher hereby disclaims any responsibility for them.

One Galleria Blvd., Suite 1900, Metairie, LA 70001
1-888-421-2397

CONTENTS

Acknowledgement v
Preface vii
Homer, Alaska 1
One Year Earlier 4
Spring Merrill Field Airport, Anchorage, Alaska 12
The Trip, First Day Airport Cafe 6:00am 16
First Day, 10:00am Entering Canada 20
First Day, 1:00pm Landing In Whitehorse, Yukon Territory 24
Prince George, British Columbia, Canada 26
2nd Day, Morning, Whitehorse 36
2nd Day 9:30am, Lake Williston 38
The Crash 40
2nd Day, Noon at the Camp 50
William Reports a Possible Accident 53
Whitehorse, Aviation People 55
2nd Day 4:00pm, Tree Platform Finished 56
William's Home, Prince George 61
2nd Day Evening in Prince George 62
2nd Day 9:00pm on the Platform 63
The Bear Attack 2nd Day 9:30pm Camp 64
3rd Day Dawn Camp 70
The Gold Find 3rd Day 8:30am Camp 73
3rd Day Noon Whitehorse 84
Phone Call to William, Prince George 85
Day 3 Mid-Day, Left Cabin, Returning to Camp 86

3rd Day, Evening, William's Home 92
3rd Day Evening, Sack Time 93
4th Day The Rescue 95
Whitehorse, Civil Air Patrol 97
Watson Lake 98
At the Gravel Airstrip 103
4th Day, Whitehorse Bound 110
Day 5, Whitehorse Lodge, Dawn 119
The Return Home 124
The Long Bus Ride to Anchorage Begins 129
Whitehorse Correctional Facility 131
The Remington Arms, Anchorage, Alaska 137
Jake Keye's Journey North 143
Trip to Whitehorse With Plane Parts 147
Home, At the Remington Arms 150
Whitehorse, Scotty's House 152
Remington Arms, Anchorage 154
Anchorage 163
Jake Keye's Journey Back Home 166
Prince George, William's House 167
Testing the Creek for Gold Potential 168
Hiking to the Cabin 171
Watson Lake 178
Back at the Camp 181
About the Author 199

ACKNOWLEDGEMENT

This story is what it is because of one special person, Judy Gross. You inspired me to write this story and to persevere to the very end. Your editing advice, humor, wit and patience meant a lot to me. You are the sunshine of my life.

PREFACE

There's no place to land. We're going to crash! That frightening experience was nearly a year ago. The memory will last a life time. This story of survival and romance and adventure is a journey that will entertain and make the reader want to read this book and visit our forty-ninth state. The author, Jack London visited Alaska, and was so inspired, he produced a few novels the world became infatuated with. The rugged appeal of adventure, pitting man against the elements and showcasing predators that challenge the food chain, plus the joy and pleasure of experiencing love again.... All of these elements will be found in this story.

A loving, committed wife, and mother, who put her heart and soul into a marriage for fifty years suddenly was left alone. No one to share the winters in the snow-bird community of Quartzsite. No one to sit next to at the holiday family gatherings. No one prepared her for life after her husband died.

A husband and father with many good memories; raising four children, standing in the trenches together, crying, laughing and giving high fives every time a hurdle was conquered; suddenly life as he knew it came to a screeching halt. A 'perfect storm' struck and the ability to continue on the same course became unbearable. Changing directions seemed like the only sane choice. Solitude was all that remained; facing the world every day alone.

Living in the grandest place on the planet was not enough; fishing, hunting and a passion for flying was not enough; God gave us arms to embrace an object; a fish, moose or majestic glacier does not quite fit the need to make one feel complete. A companion.....now that is a possibility, BUT, HOW DOES SOMEONE, NO LONGERIN THEIR PRIME, FIND A COMPANION? In the strangest places perhaps; in a crowded room? In a laundry room? What does gold and a stranger have in common? In one unguarded moment they both are pleasant to the eyes.

The pool of candidates, (companions), diminishes as the age increases. The odds of finding a soul mate, a companion, more precious than money can buy, decreases the older we get. I believe that someone in the great somewhere hears every prayer, and the heart that cries out for a companion is like a satellite that puts out a signal in every direction; somewhere, at some moment, two signals lock onto each other. The circuit is complete and both satellites begin to glow and flourish. I challenge the reader to give me a better definition of the genesis of love between two people.

This is a story whose genesis is repeated all over the globe in every society. When the signals connect there is joy and comfort. Who else but a loving God could of created such a scenario? How can someone claim He does not exist?

"YOU ARE THE LIGHT OF MY LIFE." We can say this with a happy smile when those two signals connect.

Dear Reader

This book is about two people who were knocked down for the count and decided to get up and give life another try; two people trusting God and a few strangers to heal their painful wounds and get well… one day at a time.

This is a love story, with lots of drama and action. The setting takes place in the Alaska/ Canadian wilderness. If you like survival stories you will find it hard to put this book down.

The courage to experience a new loving relationship is what this story is all about.

This is a fictional story.

HOMER, ALASKA

Our early departure from Anchorage was charged with the exciting anticipation of seeing the beautiful landscape; so much to see; the ocean on our right and the Chugach Mountains on our left; the tide flats, moose, bear, a glacier, and the pretty Kenai Mountains covered with birch and fir trees. I was hoping for a half-day fishing trip and Gail was excited about a delicious lobster-shrimp dinner.

Our weekend get-away was one year after we first met. Our room was on the second floor of a rustic white cabin, with a balcony, show casing the beautiful blue calm Katchemak Bay. A hundred miles towards the west, was the Aleutian Range of snow capped peaks. The sport fishing charters of Homer, Alaska were going back and forth out in the bay.

I had been humming the words of a song, while driving down the majestic mountainous Kenai Highway, south of Anchorage, and I could only remember the first line. I have a history of singing songs that match my euphoric moods. I knew the first line and I was curious to know if the lyrics were an accurate match for my current feelings.

"I'm glad you brought your lap top. I'm going to look up a song," I told Gail.

Using Gail's laptop, I Googled the song, 'I BELIEVE'; it was written and composed back in 1953 by four men:

Ervin Drake, Irvin Graham, Jimmy Shirl, and Al Stillman. A few of the lines that impressed me were the following;

"I believe for every drop of rain that falls, a flower grows,
And I believe that somewhere in the darkest night a candle glows.
I believe above the storm the smallest prayer will still be heard.
I believe that someone in the great somewhere hears every word.
Every time I hear a new born baby cry, or touch a leaf,
or see the sky, then I know why I believe."

"Aren't those beautiful words," I said, as I mused how accurately the words matched my feelings. Making eye contact with Gail, I said "I've lost count the many times I could have been killed; car accidents, falling off the roof of the house, falling off the top of a six foot ladder, plane accidents, grizzly encounters, hiking mishaps, playground accidents, you name it…. I'm still here. I've dodged death for a long time, and finding you is another example of a higher power intervening in my life. My life has been like a game of dodge ball with someone putting me in the right place at the right time. Do you ever slow down and reflect about where you've been, and where you are and why you feel what you feel?"

"Yeah, a little….but not like you. I mostly live and think in the present. If you ask me what my life was like when I was a child I would think about it, or reflect, as you call it….I'm not a writer, like someone who analyzes and describes their feelings. I think this is where you and I are different."

I though about what Gail said and then replied, "I never realized, until now, that everyone processes their feelings differently…. anyway, just being with you is another example of how someone, somewhere continues to bless me.

Gail was trying to process my long-winded monologue and she said, "Are you trying to tell me you're feeling grateful and you're giving God the credit for our relationship, and for helping you survive all these years in spite of lots of dumb decisions and choices?"

"Yeah….that pretty well sums it up," I said.

The bed looked so inviting. My happy, reflective mood, begged words of gratitude to God. I stared at the knotty pine open beam ceiling, as my head sunk into the soft pillow. Thank you, God, for your blessings, I thought.

"Are you excited about going for the gold?" asked Gail.

I nodded and said, "Yes. I'm ready to do some serious gold panning, scary memories and all. It's not every day a person finds a rainbow with the pot of gold included."

Gail, thinking along the rainbow theme, said, "Rainbows and real life have something in common; before the beautiful arc of colors and clear skies you have the gray turbulent ominous looking clouds. In real life, beauty and joy is usually preceded by tragedy, sadness and pain. My rainbow began to form when you caught me folding my panties in the laundry room."

"You're right; good analogy and very poetic, and reflective….So the morale of the story is look before you go into the laundry room?" I jokingly asked.

My eyes were closed, but my thoughts were far from allowing me to go to sleep. From heartache to this great weekend…Divine intervention? Why have I been so blessed? I have a wonderful companion; we survived a scary plane crash; the tree platform probably saved our lives; we found an incredible amount of gold, and a man reminded me that life is more than just working and planning every day….. Loving. Heavenly father and earthly father….Dad's life reflected a lot of His traits …the apple doesn't fall far from the tree.

ONE YEAR EARLIER

My life was just existing; like a pie without the filling. I was a lonely, angry, depressed, retired teacher, living in Anchorage, Alaska. After thirty years of marriage, and raising four children, divorce brought my life to a screeching halt.

One week-end, after months of failing to recapture peace and intimacy in our relationship, I said to my wife, "You need to get a life." Those poorly chosen words pushed our marriage over the brink….Our marriage, basically, ended that day. My four children moved with their mom to California. Like falling out of a wheel barrow, all of our lives went from feeling secure, to, OH MY GOSH, THIS IS AWFUL!

Divorce totally rearranged the closets for all of us and I felt like a lifeless form going through the motions of work, sleep and eat. I felt numb, unattached and depressed. I was angry and helpless to let go…I didn't want to let go; divorce wasn't my choice; moving on was just not happening. I was at the bottom and there was only one way to go, short of suicide, and that was find a ladder and climb it. Had we attended a divorce support group, the whole family, would have been shedding tears and asking why and who's to blame? Maybe this would of helped us. We suddenly went from a some what functional family to confusion and living a nightmare, the magnitude beyond imagination…..no band-aid was big enough to sooth the pain.

Alcohol was only a short fix and I didn't want to go down that road. A few of my uncles killed themselves with alcohol and I didn't want to take that destructive path. Church and people might help, I thought, so I visited a Baptist Church a few blocks from my house. My heart was wounded and tender. It wasn't hard for others to realize I was carrying a heavy burden; my boss, a wonderful Christian man, understood, and a few friends at work could sense the pain I was feeling. I explained to the church minister that I was recently divorced. The minister told me about a group of men, who met weekly, and that they could relate to the pain I was experiencing. The minister said I would find the support and encouragement I needed.

I visited the church men's group one evening, and after the introductions, I listened to the trials and tribulations the men were experiencing; they were hurting just like me. Two of the men had recently experienced a divorce; one man had a bi-polar sister who was about to break up his marriage, and one man was diagnosed with terminal cancer. I shared my situation and my heart erupted with a powerful flow of emotion. My tears brought tears to everyone in the room. Misery loves company I guess…no, it was more like tough times softens the heart. These men understood my pain. After one evening of dialogue with these men, I felt closer to them than my best friend at work. I looked for help in the right place; looking back, I don't believe it was luck that put me where I needed to be. They had survived, or were surviving, and this gave me a measure of encouragement. Rather than feeling like a long lost sheep, I began to sleep with the peace of knowing I wasn't alone anymore.

Looking back, I would compare divorce to a family floating on a body of water, in a rubber raft, and suddenly the craft deflates and everyone goes in different directions to try and survive. For my family, the opportunity to express and talk about our fears and confusion never happened; those early months and years went by and only time helped heal the wounded hearts. Survivors don't always talk about the dark nights and the fears of facing the world alone. The wounds healed in silence, over the months and years, for all of us. I continued teaching, but the joy of sharing my daily experiences when I got home was just not going to happen. I missed family and doing things together. For me, the lone ranger life style didn't cut it.

One day, about a year ago, my son asked me if I'd ever considered moving into a retirement community. He said the senior complexes cook all the meals and provide all kinds of recreational activities. I said, "No, I probably can't afford it." A few days after our discussion, I drove around and visited three retirement centers. The manager at the Remington Arms asked me if I was a veteran and if I'd fought in Vietnam. I said, "Yes," and then he said I could move in right away at a reduced rent, while the VA processed my case for subsidized rent and a possible pension. I had a club foot and was exposed to agent orange in the Vietnam jungle. It was to good an offer to refuse. I moved into the Remington Arms facility.

For my first meal in the dining room, I chose to sit with a man who spoke about ten words in two weeks. I decided to find another table. The couple at the second table were polite and cordial. Like a kid moving into a new community and school, I had to go through the process of finding out who I was going to be comfortable with. My second table, included a man who grew up in a mountain community and had fond memories of mountain living. My first thought was maybe this guy and I have a few things in common. I told the man and his wife a story about how I killed a moose with my hunting knife. A bull moose had been hit by a car and it's hind quarters were paralyzed. After a few gory details, describing how I killed the massive antler swinging moose, the Mrs. got up and left the table. The next day the husband explained that my moose story had ruined his wife's appetite and that I needed to be a little more discrete with the language I used. I instantly started looking for another table. I figured she probably wasn't the type that would enjoy me talking about Tom Hanks eating the raw critters on that island in the movie 'Cast Away'.

There was a threesome at another table who were always talking and laughing, and one of those ladies had a pretty smile and sparkling eyes. I noticed at their table that there was an empty seat during the three daily meals. One day, as I walked by the laundry room, I noticed the lady, with the pretty smile. I walked in and introduced myself. Hey, I thought, if she gives me a cold shoulder, so be it….what have I got to lose; she seemed to be a bit shy, but like me, she seemed to enjoy the company. I felt very comfortable conversing with this lady. She had an attractive figure. She looked too healthy to be in a retirement home. Her name was Gail Newsome. Later, Gail told me a story. She said that the first time I introduced myself, in the laundry room, she was folding her panties.... that explained why she blushed when we had our first conversation.

During the next meal, as I sipped my coffee, I noticed the empty seat again, and like responding to the word, "Go!" I walked over and said, "Excuse me. Do you mind if I join you guys?"

Gail's eyes sparkled and her smile reflected that I was welcome; that decision turned out to be a great move. The older couple, at the table, was a lovely, witty lady and her short husband. The short, ex-navy career man, had been a writer for some newspaper company over near where Ronald Reagan lived on the California coast. Two lovely ladies and two clowns; a perfect combination for an amusing dining experience. The conversation and laughter was good therapy for all of us.

Gail and I both seemed to be sizing up one another. Our relationship was probably better than any pills the psych doctor could have prescribed. Mental health and physical health are closely related. We didn't need a doctorate degree to figure that out. Each new day brought more sunshine into our lives as we both looked forward to starting the day sitting together and laughing about things at the dining room table. Conversation on a wide range of subjects was becoming the norm. Our listening skills and daily schedules were being fine tuned to accommodate the strong attraction we were both feeling. The rumor was we were fast becoming the new "love birds" at the Remington. We knew everyone was talking about us...that was ok. We must have reflected that glow that love birds exude.

We learned we had a lot in common: children, camping, boating and RVing. I learned she and her husband played different kinds of board games, and for years she kept an accurate count of their wins and losses. I thought that was a neat thing to do; it showed a competitive spirit that I related too. We both got involved in several games weekly and she kept score. It seemed the more we talked about our lives, and shed a few tears, along with a lot of laughs, that life got sweeter. Physical contact was a natural progression as our relationship became more treasured. I was a touchy person long before I met Gail, and to put my hand on her shoulder or to touch her when it was time to go to our separate rooms felt so natural and comfortable. One evening, not long after we met I gave Gail a soft kiss standing by her door. She was receptive, and from that evening on, kisses and hugs were part of the highly charged electricity that was part of our blossoming relationship.

The Remington Arms family seemed like a microcosm of society; there were those who were depressed and spaced- out, and a few who were cheerful, smiling and friendly. There was also a few who seemed to have a cynical attitude that even the best couch psych probably couldn't unravel. Bitterness is one sad pathway; one can only guess why an individual ends up being an introverted cynic; one resident said, "We get cynical because we don't get what we want." Abby would probably advise us to avoid the toxic cynics of the world. Many of the residents were recently widowed and this would explain why sad faces were a common site. Life is a struggle for everyone, especially those who lose a spouse. The positive, cheerful residents, in spite of age or handicap, were like sixty-watt bulbs lighting up the hallways and dining room. The raw reality of old age is revealed every day in a rest home or even in an Independent Living facility. It is so sad to see a man or woman who has lost a spouse of fifty years or more. It's a difficult transition of adjusting to living the remainder of one's life without that warm body to cuddle up next to at night, or to laugh with when someone says or does something funny. Living alone, eventually, is a fate most of us will face, and seeing this struggle play out every day is a heavy dose of reality. Finding a soul mate of a friend at any age is a blessing that cannot be measured. Like seeing two doves paired together…it's a beautiful scene.

Every human spirit has a breaking point. For the compassionate, friendly Gail, her weary fight to nurse her ailing husband broke her spirit. The labor of love for a five year period was grueling; trips to the hospital or doctor appointments; being the chauffeur every day lifting the wheel chair in and out of the vehicle and trying to be patient and cheerful to a man who often felt down and depressed was a heavy challenge. Soon after her husband died, she experienced a complete mental and physical breakdown; her will to live and love evaporated. She lost a third of her body weight. She felt trapped in a body that didn't care about family or life. Her kids brought food in and drove her for doctor appointments. Joy was totally void in her life. Her supporting soul mate was gone. Her purpose for living was gone. Her children talked it over and decided a retirement home would be the safest and healthiest place for their Mom to live. They checked out the Remington Arms and decided the prepared meals and maid service and recreational activities would best fit mom's needs.

New walls didn't improve Gail's depressed soul; she still refused to leave her one bedroom apartment. The strength of character that Gail had inherited was also equally strong at keeping her in the doldrums. She refused to leave her apartment. Resurrection, for Gail, occurred as a result of a few persistent women who insisted she come down to the dining room. A few of these women left their spouses and sat with her. The loving group won out. Gail received lots of hugs and kisses from the ladies. It was a slow process, but each day the scales tipped from despair and no hope, to laughter and smiles. I came along, and into Gail's life, about six months after she moved into the Remington Arms.

Gail had been a take-charge, go the extra mile type nurse for twenty plus years. She worked for a small town doctor who had trained her to assist him with nearly everything except IVs and surgery; basically she was a precursor to our current nurse practitioner without the title or pay grade. She was appreciated for her skills and faithful support; along with her job she was the mother of two sons and a daughter. Balancing work, motherhood and marriage was no easy task. Her family went the popular route from tent camping and boating to the tent trailer, to the trailer, to the recreational vehicles. Years of fun filled memories of the family camping trips were stored away, and now, at the Remington, new experiences were being deposited; life was not over…a new chapter was just beginning.

I had been a teacher for thirty plus years; not bad for having a mother who thought college was not in the cards for her son. I was a country boy. Dad was a farm laborer, the first eight years of my life, and working in the fields was part of my education. Entertaining myself was also a way of life that influenced my social skills. I never integrated very comfortably into the social party scene. Living in the country didn't present a lot of opportunities to mix with boys and girls my age. I was a pretty shy kid growing up, especially around girls. No one in our family, except a distant aunt, had ever gone to college. I was an academic no-show in school. I only desired to excel in sports. The competitive spirit remained dormant as far as academics were concerned, but in sports I erupted and made a big splash in a small pond. Towards the end of high school reality kicked in. How was I going to feed myself, since mom and Dad were about to give me an eviction notice. My self-esteem was good; my self-confidence was good. I was use to setting goals in sports, and reaching those goals. What I lacked was confidence in the classroom. I made a decision that startled my parents. I decided to go to college to become a Physical Education teacher. What a whirl wind adventure that was. I shared my college days, after Vietnam, with the love of my life, my first wife. We both cracked the books and became teachers. We taught in California, Arizona and Alaska. Four children came along in the next ten years; three girls and one boy. My childhood included a lot of camping, hunting and fishing trips. Dad, a faithful hard worker, followed sports, and mom loved the mountains and fishing. So much of what gave joy and pleasure to my parents rubbed off on me. My parents worked hard during the week, but on weekends we had fun. Funny how those early years set the pattern for my life. It wasn't perfect, my childhood, but it was balanced and laced with many good memories of bragging about who won the hearts game or who caught the most fish.

Gail and her husband raised one daughter and two sons. We both grew up in rural, small communities. Along with cheerleading, Gail worked evenings at a drive-in theatre. She loved school. She and her mother had a wonderful relationship. No topic was off-limits. She was the big sister of five brothers. Responsibilities were a big part of her early childhood. Putting up with and keeping five brother rug rats out of harms way was not easy. As a child, Gail walked through the Mojave Desert to get to school every day; she was no stranger to rattle snakes. We both shared our out-house stories, plus the glorious break through day when we finally got a flush toilet.

We were both busy trying to keep our heads above water, so to speak, when our paths crossed. Companionship was something we both desperately needed; over the next several months, Gail and I became close friends. I told her I was a pilot and that flying was one of my few passions. She made it clearly known that flying was one of her worst fears.

As our relationship grew stronger, her resistance to a plane ride weakened. One day, early in the spring, Gail said to me, "I've lived a full life and I'm not going to live forever, so I may as well see if I can get comfortable in your plane."

"Really?" I replied.

I told her that I would let her know if I was going to make any turns or climbs or descents.

"OK. I'll give it a try." she said.

SPRING MERRILL FIELD AIRPORT, ANCHORAGE, ALASKA

The next sunny day that came along, we visited the airport. I was biting at the bit to entertain and show off my flying toy. The narrow entrance to the airport presented hangars on the right and a wide assortment of tied down single engine aircraft on the left. Half of the approximately one hundred and fifty planes were tail-draggers, meaning they had tail wheels, which are designed for short field gravel strips. The colors and various high-wing and low-wing planes were quite a spectacle to a first time visitor. Most of the people traveling from the bush choose to park at Merrill Field, on the northwest side of Anchorage. The big commercial aircraft use the large international strip. There is no rule forbidding the small planes from landing on the huge international strip, but common sense dictates that Merrill Field is safer and more user friendly for small planes. The big aircraft have been known to flip over small planes when they add thrust for a departure; also it is a little discomforting having a monster plane going 180 miles per hour coming up on your rear end just before touching down.

When we pulled up to my plane I gave Gail a choice of staying in the car or walking around the plane, as I did the preflight check; she stayed in the car. I could tell she was nervous. After the check, I signaled for her to come and get into the cockpit.

The cockpit was as alien to Gail, as sitting in a flying saucer. She was afraid to touch anything, especially the yoke, which is similar to the steering wheel in a car. The dash had a wide assortment of gauges, and she guessed that eventually I would explain their purpose and function. I locked up the car and untied the ropes that secured the plane. After climbing into the cockpit I took the preflight list and went through the numbers, checking the controls and instruments.

I looked at Gail to prepare her for the noise that would come from the engine. "Starting the engine will be just like starting a car engine... nothing to be alarmed about, Ok?" Gail nodded her chin. We slowly drove over to the run way. Gail's knuckles were white as she remained silent. The actual ride on the ground is slightly bumpier in a plane than in a quality car and this alone is enough to raise the level of concern for a first time passenger. In front of the tower I announced that I was ready to taxi for take-off. The tower operator gave me permission to taxi; after checking the magnetos I announced I was ready to depart. The tower responded with an "All clear."

"When the plane reaches sixty miles per hour we will gently lift off the ground and climb slowly up in the air.....it will be perfectly smooth." I said, as the engine roared and the wheels rolled along to the take-off speed of sixty knots.

As the plane came off the asphalt, I said, "Now when we get about five hundred feet up I will make a gentle left turn." Gail took a deep breath as the plane steadily climbed to five hundred feet above the city streets. Looking down, when I first flew in a small plane, was a bit intimidating for me, and I got the feeling when the wing dropped in a turn, that Gail also felt a bit uncomfortable. Before each turn I explained what I was going to do; Gail didn't appear to be overly nervous and there was no problem with air sickness.

From five hundred feet up we could see the tide was out in the Cook Inlet. The main roads around town were busy with folks commuting to work. The Chugach Mountains, that climbed swiftly north of town, were still blanketed with snow. The sun reflected off the mountain peaks with a bright white radiance that always impressed tourists arriving at the Anchorage International Airport.

When we got on the ground I took a deep breath and said, "How was it?"

"Ok, smoother than riding in a car. The landing made me nervous. I felt like we were going to plow right into the ground until you lifted the nose and glided to the ground; after the wheels hit I was ok."

"Good. That last phase of the landing is the part that discourages some people from getting their license; a few never get comfortable with the flair just before the wheels touch the asphalt," I said, thinking, one small step for her and one major step for our relationship.

Winter was transitioning into spring. Green was cropping up everywhere. The days were getting longer and with each good weather day I got more and more antsy to take a trip. "Cabin fever", especially in Alaska, is a common problem, for out-doors people like myself.

One day, while listening to the weather report in Gail's apartment, I asked her if she would be interested in flying with me down to Prince George, British Columbia, to visit my son and daughter-in law. I said it would be about a one week trip. I pulled out a map and showed her the route, which paralleled the Alaska-Canadian highway.

"Might be fun. What would your kids think?" asked Gail.

"What do you mean?"

"Would they object to us being together?"

I thought for a few seconds and then said, "Well, no. They just want us to be happy." "It might be fun," grinned Gail.

"Think about it," I said, with an optimistic guess that she might accept the invitation.

For a week Gail thought about the invitation. All of my adult life, with one man. For fifty years it was 'us' everyday. My whole world revolved around him.....how to please him and care for him. I am free to move on....Free...like a bird outside it's cage. Thanks to Bill, I'm beyond coping. I feel like I did when I was a blushing bride. Each new day seems to bring less pain and more joy. My heart is begging me to step out of my comfort zone. A little voice seems to be saying, I DARE YOU TO LOVE AGAIN. It's scary, but I feel safe; it's exciting; he has a kind, sensitive and gentle nature; a new life, a new love, and in addition, I can still keep my fifty plus years of memories......He would want me to be happy, and to seek the desire of my heart, thought Gail.

Later in the day Gail smiled, as the thought crossed her mind...I think I'll take his offer.

"Go ahead and pick a date for that trip. Your co-pilot has decided to go," said Gail.

"Super!" was the only word I chose to describe my pleasure.

I checked with my son's wife, Stephannie, a school teacher, off for the summer break, and she said the best time to visit was the second week in June.

We discussed what to take and decided eighty pounds worth of baggage was the limit. The survival gear took up the rest of the weight that the plane would allow, including the maximum amount of gas. Gail suggested we pick up two Alaska t-shirts for the kids.

The recreational activities at the Remington Arms kept us busy, plus several more short flying trips. The beautiful Matanuska Valley of Wasilla and Palmer, with a beautiful pine-fir mix forest and luscious green pasture land, was only a twenty minute flight north of Anchorage. The Big Lake, Palmer and Wasilla airstrips were good places to go and practice landings, and even walk a short distance for a hamburger. Gail was getting more familiar and comfortable with the sounds in the cockpit, plus the g-forces when the plane made a turn or ascended; little did either of us know what we were going to experience in a few more weeks.

One day, during lunch, I told Gail a true story about an Alaska couple; the husband was a pilot of a four passenger Cessna. The two of them were flying into Anchorage one day when he had a fatal heart attack. The wife had recently completed a survivor's course in the basics of flying. The instructor, who taught the course, was on duty in the Merrill Field Airport tower when the wife took the radio and announced her dilemma. She declared that her husband was incapacitated and that she needed help to land the plane. The tower operator recognized her voice and between the two of them she successfully got the plane on the ground. The Survivor Course probably saved her life. Gail said she would try and learn the basics, such as working the throttle, using the radio, making gentle turns and descending and ascending. Our short trips gave her practice and further increased her confidence and level of security.

THE TRIP, FIRST DAY
AIRPORT CAFE 6:00AM

Our departure date finally arrived—bags packed; we were ready to go. I knocked lightly on Gail's apartment door at 6:00 o'clock. We drove to the cafe adjacent to the Merrill Field airport. Gail had her hash browns, biscuits and gravy and I had French toast. There were a few other patrons, but we didn't recognize anyone. I was pumped thinking about the trip. The icing on the cake was my co-pilot. God's perfect piece of art was when He brought a man and a woman together. The chemistry I felt being with Gail has tried to be described by poets for centuries. Complete seems to be the one word that comes close to describing how I felt in Gail's presence; joy, contented, happy; all these feelings blended together as we were about to fly the pretty skies of Alaska.

In the restaurant I looked at Gail and said, "Pinch me." She smiled and wrinkled her eyebrows. She reached across the table and pinched my extended arm. "Ok, I just had to make sure this is not a dream. I can't believe we are going to do this."

We arrived at the plane at 6:55; ten minutes later we were in the cockpit.

"I hope Harold finds your car," said Gail.

"He has a cell phone if there is any problem."

Merrill Field, arguably one of the busiest small plane airports in the world, was quiet except for one plane that was rolling full throttle down the strip. We probably were the control tower operator's second customer of the day.

The weather report called for sunny skies. The first thirty minutes of our flight took us north to the beautiful, wooded-farm communities of Wasilla and Palmer. I squeezed Gail's hand.

"You ok?" I asked. Gail smiled and nodded her head. She had that serious, concentrating look of a good co-pilot. The tide water was out in the inlet and the mud flats exposed drift wood everywhere. The upper banks revealed several moose and their calves. The beautiful Palmer Hospital, near the highway outside of Palmer, shown in the morning sun. The thick green forest of Wasilla revealed early morning plumes of smoke from the many homes hidden in the dense woods. The morning temperature was still in the mid-thirties.

We left the flat country soon after we passed over the Palmer Air Strip and began to make a slow climb in order to stay a few thousand feet above the Glenn Highway.

"We'll be in the Talkeetna Mountains in a few minutes and we might get some small bumps."

"We'll be flying over Victory Bible Camp in a little while. My kids went there in the summer. Check out the rapids." Directly below us was a tumbling, silty gray fed, glacial river.

"That's the Matanuska River. They give guided rafting trips on that section of the river." "Is that a glacier over there?" Gail asked, as she pointed ahead and to the right.

"Yes. That's the Matanuska Glacier; see the dark debris on top of the glacier? The crevasses and jagged ice ridges on the surface make a safe landing on the glacier impossible." The dark blue ice leading edge of the glacier was enormously high. The water at the base of the glacier had a gray silty appearance.

We were a half mile above the winding highway. The view was fantastic: far superior to that of the people driving their cars below. I felt grateful that I had a plane and that I could get out once in a while and see the world from an eagle's perspective.

Gail pointed out a plane coming our way; it dipped its wings and I told Gail, "Take the yoke and say Hi." Like a trooper, she took the yoke and rocked the wings. We waved at the passengers in the other plane. We were close enough to see their smiles as they quickly flew out of sight. I was beaming with joy, as I watched Gail holding onto the yoke and letting go with her right hand and waving at the people in the other plane.

"I'm impressed. A few months ago you were afraid of touching any part of the plane," I said. Gail blushed as our smiling eyes met.

Further ahead in the distance, a mountain peak, with a notch like the front sights of a rifle, came into view. "That's Gun Sight Pass, and when we get there, the terrain opens up and we'll be able to see a hundred miles in every direction." There were a few lodges below for travelers to spend a night and get a good meal. The few lodges I had visited were very rustic looking, with huge open beamed ceilings and mounted trophies nailed to the walls. The terrain was fairly level from our perspective; commonly referred to as tundra country; a popular caribou habitat.

"We're in caribou country now. The caribou usually walk in single file as they travel across the tundra."

A few minutes later Gail spotted half a dozen caribou walking along the edge of a snow covered lake. "I see some caribou! There's a pack of wolves following them."

"Cool," Gail said, as I gently banked the plane and went down for a closer look. The white snow covered lake made the long single file of animals clearly visible from a long distance.

"Do you think the wolves will be able to catch them?" Gail asked.

"No. Healthy caribou can travel a hundred miles a day," I replied.

Danny, check me out; I'm in a small airplane, and loving every minute of it, thought Gail, as she silently spoke to her deceased husband…He's a nice man…you would approve, thought Gail.

We were about ninety minutes into the trip; ahead of us was the sleepy, little town of Glennallen. The forest was very thick with Sitka Spruce. The flight above the highway took us right over the heart of the small community. The city received it's name after two military explorers, Captain Glenn and Lieutenant Allen. The town was a base camp during WW ll while the highway to Anchorage was under construction.. The five hundred residents are about a two hour drive to either Fairbanks or Anchorage. The summer weather can go as high as eighty and the winter temperature can drop as low as minus 50 degrees Fahrenheit. The houses were well hidden in the thick forest. Like Wasilla, there were plumes of smoke spiraling up into the sky from the roof tops. As we passed over the houses I spotted several large dogs on short chains outside of their wooden shelters. I felt sorry for the dogs. The small breeds are kept in the house during the winter but the larger thick-haired dogs, that are commonly used for pulling sleds, are chained outside, near their small shelter. Life in bush Alaska is not easy for man or beast.

FIRST DAY, 10:00AM
ENTERING CANADA

Two plus hours into the flight we were approaching the small community of Northway, population, approximately a hundred people. I declared to the Northway air traffic that we were arriving. The terrain was incredibly level as we looked at the highway winding through the forest, my bladder was about to burst from the breakfast juices. Northway is near the U.S. Canadian border.

"Cross your fingers. We're going to be inspected by the Canadian Customs Agent when we land. A few years ago one agent made me completely empty my plane. Look for the man in a white shirt."

There were no planes in the Northway pattern and we had a nice, soft landing. The strip looked like it needed a fresh coat of asphalt; there were a lot of cracks developing. The temperature was a chilly 34 degrees. Northway is noted for extremely cold winters and cool summers.

"Here he comes," I said, as I parked the plane near the white wooden Customs building. The approaching agent was wearing a white, well pressed, long sleeve shirt that exposed a big beer belly. He looks like the same agent that made me unload the plane on the last trip, I thought. He had his clip board in one hand. I got out and walked around and helped Gail get down to the asphalt.

"Good morning," I said to the inspector. My bladder was now begging relief and I was in a near panic situation. I could barely control my bladder.

We were asked a few questions, like destination, pets, fruit, handguns, terrorist explosives; most of the answers were NO…..

"Ok, I hope you have a safe, enjoyable trip." Oh Lord, help me to hold it a little longer, I thought.

"Thank you," I said, as I took Gail's hand and headed for the cafe. I headed for the men's restroom.

Gail looked at some of the native art. A few minutes later we spotted a beaver hat; the price was $ 225.00. I told Gail twenty years earlier my old beaver hat had only cost fifty bucks.

"Do you want anything?" I asked.

"I'll split a milkshake with you."

"Sure. How about some water to go along with our sandwiches and chips?"

"We walked over to the Customs building and left a flight plan for Whitehorse. The Canadian border was thirty minutes down the road.

Leaving Northway, as far as we could see, the shiny green blanket of trees seemed to have a downward slope to it. Gail broke out the sandwiches and potato chips. We were making good time. We would probably arrive at Whitehorse by 1:30 P.M. Whitehorse was our stopping place for the day.

Gail spotted a pack of wolves feeding on a carcass….either a caribou or a moose most likely, I thought.

I pointed out that Valdez was over to our right a good hundred miles and that the Yukon River was over to the left about two hundred miles. So far the ride was dead calm; no forest fire smoke or a storm front that might indicate turbulence or visibility problems. Gail seemed totally engrossed in the rivers and lakes below. I pointed at one of the instruments and said, "This instrument will tell me within a tenth of a mile, the distance to Whitehorse."

"Would you mind calling Harold and ask him if he found the car? Click on people and you'll find his number." "Hello." answered Harold.

"Hi. This is Gail. How are you doing?"

"Fine. How is it with you guys?" asked Harold.

"So far it's been a beautiful trip. Were you able to find the car?" asked Gail. "It's tucked away in the garage. Margaret got mad at me today during lunch." "Why?" asked Gail.

"I tried to close the dining room blinds and she shouted at me and said, 'No! Go sit down!' "I don't like her," said Harold.

"Stay away from Margaret."

"Tell Bill I said to drive careful," said Harold.

"I will. Thanks for taking care of the car."

"No problem."

"Ok, we'll see you in about a week, bye," chuckled Gail.

"What's so funny?" I asked.

"Harold had an argument with Margaret over the window blinds."
"Why?"

She was enjoying the sunshine and Harold wanted some shade."

I smiled and shook my head. "Sounds like he stirred up a wild cat. How old is Harold?" I asked.

"Ninety two." Harold was one of our faithful card players. He had the shingles pretty bad and sometimes he got pretty grumpy with the female employees. Gail picked up chocolate candy at the store for him every couple of weeks and this kept him on our good side.

"The car is locked and parked in it's usual space," said Gail.

The scattered cars on the highway were reflecting the bright sunlight.

"I've got to show you something." I made a slow right turn and the animals came into sight, directly below Gail's window. There's a pack of wolves in pursuit of a moose.

"Oh I wish we could help her." The five wolves had the moose totally surrounded and there was no escape. The wolves were nipping at the moose's legs; they would eventually fatigue the fifteen hundred pound animal until it could no longer defend itself. In the wilderness there are no referees. This battle was going to be won by patience, perseverance and wits, checkmate. I shrugged my shoulders; Gail shook her head.

"We've got another hour; look over there!" I said, as I lowered the nose and pointed at the ground directly ahead. I spotted a grizzly and two cubs. I nosed down the plane and flew over the bears at about five hundred feet. The mother bear stood up on her hind legs and the two cubs parked themselves between mamma's two huge hairy legs. Like

King Kong of the tundra, she had her paws moving like, come and try to get me sucker. She could see that the plane was approaching and she was in an attack posture.

"I wouldn't want to be there on the ground right now. Did you see those angry red eyes?" I replied.

Seeing this bear stand her ground reminded me of the moose carnage on the railroad tracks between Anchorage and Denali Park in the winter of 1985. Moose, very often, in the winter, refuse to get off the tracks when a train comes along. A huge fast approaching train, blaring it's horn, does not always intimidate the largest member of the deer family. The moose prefer to walk the tracks rather than plow through the deep snow. During the winter of 1985 there were over three hundred train/moose encounters; the train always wins.

My cockpit instrument indicated we were thirty seven miles out of Whitehorse.

FIRST DAY, 1:00PM
LANDING IN WHITEHORSE, YUKON TERRITORY

The quiet city of Whitehorse sits on a flat shelf of land on the banks of the Yukon River. Most of the 28,000 residents of the Yukon Territory reside in Whitehorse. The summers in Whitehorse bristle with recreational activity. Rafting, kayak and canoe activities and ATV trails and cross country bike races, hiking, camping and fishing galore. There's a large number of dining establishments. The local college has year round courses and hosts a wide choice of plays and musical entertainment. With a good job, Whitehorse is a fine community to raise a family or simply hang one's shingle.

Maybe this evening we can go to that steak restaurant, I thought. "Would you be interested in eating a buffalo steak this evening?" "Sure. I've eaten a buffalo hamburger before," said Gail.

"A friend told me about a place called the Klondike Rib and Salmon Restaurant; the Bison steaks are excellent. We'll have time for a nap before dinner."

"I'm not tired," said Gail.

"Ok I'll let you carry the heavy luggage over to the lodge." Gail had a quick comeback; "No you won't! You're suppose to treat me like a lady."

"Opps. You might have to remind me once in a while…..I'm kind of out of practice."

"I'll do that," replied Gail, reflecting a determined smile.

"We have twenty more miles; would you look up the frequency for the Whitehorse tower?" Gail wrote down the frequency on a post-it and stuck it on the yoke. I switched one radio to the Whitehorse frequency and immediately picked up radio traffic.

PRINCE GEORGE, BRITISH COLUMBIA, CANADA

"Hello honey, any word from Dad?" asked William, Bill's son, calling from work.

"No." answered Stephannie.

"I'm tempted to see if I can get him on his cell phone," William replied.

"Go ahead," Stephannie answered.

All of my four kids were a little anxious about their Dad flying hundreds of miles through the Rocky Mountain wilderness. William was newly hired to work for a Nissen dealership in Prince George. He had recently graduated with honors from a vocational auto school. He and his wife Stephannie, a Canadian middle school teacher, were in the fast lane of young careers, and enjoying life. They were hoping to have children sometime in the future.

"Hello," I answered.

"Where are you?" asked William.

"We're about fifteen miles out of Whitehorse. We're going to stop there and get an early morning start. My co-pilot is doing a good job of navigating," I said, as I patted Gail on the knee.

"Will you be in Prince George tomorrow afternoon?"

"Weather permitting," I said.

"Our weather is forecast to be good tomorrow," said William.

"Good. I'll get a weather report in the morning before we leave. If things are marginal I'll give you a call. We are flying down the Trench, along the Lake Williston shoreline. There are only a few gravel strips along the route, so I will fly only if it looks good. I figure we'll be there close to 4:00 o'clock in the afternoon."

"Sounds good. I was thinking about all of us going out for dinner," said William.

"That sounds good."

"Be careful, have fun," said William.

"Love you guys, bye."

"We'll be seeing Whitehorse any minute. The cell towers have really improved communication. This is the first trip for me to be able to talk on the cell phone. The world is getting smaller all the time," I said.

The city smoke was visible up ahead.

"Whitehorse Tower, this is Cessna 52843; five miles northwest of Whitehorse."

"52843 this is Whitehorse Tower."

"This is 52843, requesting to land."

"Roger 52843. You are cleared to land on runway 090."

"52843, thank you."

"52843, requesting you close my flight plan."

"Roger 52843."

"The restroom is in the tower; need to go?" I asked.

"Good idea."

I grabbed the two suit cases and we headed towards the tall blue building.

"Check out that plane." I was talking about a World War ll, DC-3 plane that was mounted on a 24 inch metal post. It actually functions like a huge windsock and the nose always points into the wind. As we walked by the huge plane I looked ahead and measured the last hundred yards of asphalt before we reached the lodge. I was glad we were traveling light.

The lodge looks the same, I thought; no new paint. I hope they still have the coffee shop.

The restaurant was still intact; no customers, lots of empty booths. The clerk's desk was located near the hall way that led to a half dozen rooms.

"Can we get a room for one night?" I asked.

The young male clerk said, "No problem; would a queen bed be ok?" "Do you have two twins?"

"We can roll in a cot," said the clerk.

"That'll be fine."

As we walked down the carpeted hallway, I thought, maybe I should have asked her about the bed arrangement. "Was the cot idea ok with you?"

"Who gets the bed?" chuckled Gail.

"We'll flip a coin. No, I'm kidding. You can have the bed," I said.

We put our suit cases in the room, and after checking out the bathroom we both crashed on the bed. I looked at my watch…2:00 o'clock PM.

"What shall we do? We have three or four hours before dinner." "Your nap idea sounds good," said Gail.

"Would you like to check out that steak restaurant and see some of the town?" I asked.

"Sure…maybe we could do some window shopping."

Gail curled into a fetal position with her head on the soft pillow. "I enjoyed the flight but it feels good to be back on the ground. I'm looking forward to going into town," said Gail.

"Me too. I like to hear the Canadian accent."

Gail looked into my eyes and smiled and said, "Good-nap."

Nearly two hours later we both got up refreshed and excited about heading into town.

"I'll go see if I can get the number for a cab and see if the Klondike Restaurant is still in business."

I came back a few minutes later and said that the lodge clerk got off work in thirty minutes and that he volunteered to drive us to the restaurant.

In the lodge cafe there were some postcards and a bulletin board with miscellaneous job announcements and items for sale. I showed Gail the postcard of the popular Whitehorse tourist attraction, The Klondike.

"That's a huge, white paddle-wheeler that is now dry docked on high ground next to the Yukon River; long ago it hauled passengers and freight up and down the Yukon River. The larger paddle boats were wide and two hundred feet long; they were shallow draft boats designed to glide near the surface of the shallow swift rivers. Imagine the excitement of the native people when that big baby came by the villages. The paddle boat captains had an awesome responsibility navigating the Yukon. Fifteen hundred miles of countless twisting bends and shallow sandbars required a lot of skill and savvy to stay out of trouble."

We decided to sit in one of the cafe booths and have a coke.

"I'm sure glad you came along," I said, almost blushing, as my joy of contentment over flowed.

"I'm having a good time, thank you. I feel a little sore and stiff from sitting, but a couple of aspirin will fix that. Do you think we'll be able to get down to Prince George tomorrow?" Gail asked quickly, hoping she could mask her joy that was about to split at the seam.

"If the weather stays like it was today, we will be there in time for supper." Could she land the plane if something happened to me? I thought.

"The Federal Aviation Authority in the USA does not require a back-up pilot in all planes but it is a good thing to always have someone who can take over in case the pilot has a health issue. I feel you could probably land this plane safely if it became necessary…so here's the deal, prove me right, let's do some role playing," I said. Gail looked at me with a smile and thought….. Oh boy, where are we going with this?

"Pretend we are in the plane and I pass out; we are at 5,000 feet above the highway, coming into Whitehorse. Tell me, step-by-step, what would you do?"

"Umm," said Gail, as she thought about the question….." I would take the steering wheel, I mean yoke, and make sure the plane stayed level; I would fly towards the airport and key the mike and say, Help!; I would explain that you passed out and I need help; I would wait for instructions from the tower; I would squeeze the throttle and push it in and out to get use to working it; I would keep the speed at 70 or higher and slowly lower the nose towards the runway; slowly working the pedals to keep the plane straight; pull the throttle all the way out when the wheels hit the runway; tap the top of the peddles to slow down the plane; when I got stopped I would tell the tower to call an ambulance for both of us." We both laughed at that last comment.

"Wow!" I beamed with pride. "You're a good student, or am I a good teacher?" "Maybe a little of both," said Gail, with a high noon glow on her face.

As Gail sipped on her coke, she commented, "Feel a little more secure now?" said Gail with a smile.

"Much more," I said.

"When you stepped out I tuned on the news, and they were debating whether women should be allowed to fight side by side with men in combat. What do you think?" asked Gail.

"If it were the Alamo where the Texans were vastly out numbered, I would say yes, but in todays world, like in Iraq, I would say no. I think women can compete with men flying a jet or a helicopter, but side by side, or building to building on the ground…no. Women would be a distraction, and men might use poor judgment if a female comrade were to get into trouble. The sexual aspect could cause problems also. What do you think?" I asked.

"I wouldn't want my husband in a foxhole with a woman….If you put twenty men in a hot lonely desert outpost under a big tent with a refrigerator full of ice cream and cookies, sooner or later one of the men would sneak over and sample some of the goodies," said Gail.

"I don't understand why women would want to have the option… just like in sports; why do they insist on playing football with the boys? Men don't demand that they be allowed to race against the women or play on a women's basketball team. I never enjoyed seeing girls compete with the guys in wrestling, but this has been happening for years. A few loud squeaky idiots have tried to squeeze a round object into a square hole, and the silent lambs of the world have allowed a few to play out a train wreck scenario that flops from the get go."

"When you were in Vietnam did you see women in combat roles?" asked Gail

"No. I saw women nurses in the hospital when I was recovering from my leg wound, but that was the only place." "How did you get hurt?" asked Gail.

"I was a radio operator and a sniper shot me while I was riding in a jeep. The bullet went through my calf muscle just behind the bone. I was in the hospital for two weeks and then was sent back to my company. The captain assigned me to permanent duty at the headquarters company. I never went out in the field again. I didn't complain." The café waitress was a woman in her late sixties and I couldn't help but feel sorry for her. What a shame, I thought. A person her age still has to get out of bed at five o'clock and trudge down to a restaurant and wait on customers. Canada is no different than the U.S.; retirement income just doesn't cut it. Gail and I were fortunate in that we were getting a pension that allowed us to live relatively comfortable.

"Did you say your son-in-law was a sheriff?" I asked.

"Bryan, yes," answered Gail.

"I bet he trained himself to expand his awareness of the movement of people and individuals within his field of vision ….I was in line at the bank, the other day, and I noticed a man, maybe in his thirties; clean cut and scanning everybody around me. I figured he was an off-duty cop."

"I remember Brian saying he was constantly having to fill out reports, and he had to be accurate in detail and sequence; like what happened, and where, and when.

"Makes sense," I said. I looked at the people in the cafe….. "If you closed your eyes could you describe everyone in here now?"

Gail closed her eyes. "You, me, the waitress, three people in one booth; a boy, man and a woman…..that's all."

Gail looked around and saw that she missed three other patrons; she shrugged her shoulders.

"My grandson, Kevin, had a talk with me one day about being aware of people in parking lots and the mall. He's a police officer, like his Dad." Gail replied, proudly.

"It's a tough job," I said. I looked at my watch. "I'll go see if the clerk is ready to leave."

Gail watched me walk away and thought, Is this what it feels like to be courted by a knight in shiny armor? Was that an expression of contentment, she asked herself.

The clerk saw me approach and said, "Give me a second. I've got to clock-out."

It was a two mile drive into town. The kid drove us right up to the restaurant door. I handed the young man five bucks, but he refused to take the money. "No, I had to come this way anyway. My house is only a few blocks away."

"Well, ok. Thank you." I said.

"Nice kid," I said to Gail, as we walked into the restaurant. "He refused to take my tip."

The atmosphere in the steakhouse was definitely frontier. The pine rafters and stuffed animals on the walls; the enlarged photographs of prospectors and the river boats......history everywhere. The waitress said the building was the oldest restaurant in town. My buffalo steak was a tad dry; about somewhere between moose and beef. The sauce and baked buttery potatoes complemented the meat. The patrons at one table within ear shot sounded American.

"Are you folks from the lower forty-eight?" I asked.

"We're RVing from Colorado to Alaska," said one of the men. They were three couples in their sixties, I'd guess. We introduced ourselves. It's always interesting to share vacation stories with other people. We were invited to pull our table over closer so we could share stories of our journey. They had family in Alaska. Their trip so far was very interesting; no mechanical problems. They were anxious to get to Anchorage. We told them we were flying and that we left Anchorage about ten hours earlier. They seemed a bit envious when the word airplane was mentioned.

"Are you folks retired?" I asked. They said they had a few more years to go and that they were looking forward to it. It was interesting to find out two of the women were teachers. When I mentioned that I had taught school in a few native villages the ladies had several questions about schools and education in rural Alaska. An hour later we excused ourselves and headed out the door.

"That was fun," said Gail as we stepped out into the afternoon sunlight.

"It sounds like they are having fun. Did it remind you of your Quartzite RV trips?" I asked.

"Yes it did," said Gail.

"I'm stuffed," I said, as I patted my stomach, on the sidewalk outside of the restaurant.

"We should of ordered one plate and split it," said Gail. "Would you like to walk around for a while?"

"I'd love to," I said.

The Klondike boat was visible down the street, nearly a quarter of a mile away. We decided to window shop in that direction. The street reminded me of downtown Anchorage. The many little shops provided a variety of merchandise. Neither one of us were looking for anything in particular...especially food. We walked up close to the big boat. It was a work of art. The three walking decks and the windows and cabin doors were designed by a master craftsman. The Yukon River was about a hundred yards away. The powerful current, about a hundred yards wide, was a beautiful clear, dark blue color. I imagined being in a canoe floating down that powerful current heading towards Dawson and the Klondike gold country, clear out to the mouth of the Yukon at the shore of the Bering Sea.

I pulled out my convenient cell phone and called a cab. In five minutes we were on our way back to the lodge.

"Where you folks from?" asked the cabbie.

"Anchorage."

"I've been there; nice town; I flew from there to visit my sister in Los Angeles." "What did you think of the traffic in L.A.?" I asked.

"No thank-you; dog eat dog attitude down there; the weather was nice, but it's way to crowded for me....Are you driving down the Cassiar?"

"We're flying my Cessna down to Prince George," I replied.

"Wow! Do you have room for one more? Just kidding," said the cabbie.

What a perfect way to end a perfect day, I thought, as I looked up at the pretty blue sky.

"I think I'll call Joni when we get in our room. It's been a lovely day and I can't remember having so much fun," said Gail. Gail thought, I'm having the kind of day that makes me want to shout it to the whole world.

"Maybe I'll call one of my kids too," I said.

A line from the movie, 'South Pacific' came to Gail's mind….'I'm in love, I'm in love, I'm in love with a wonderful guy.'

"Hello," answered Gail's daughter, Joni.

"Hi babe. We're on the ground in Whitehorse."

"Mom, I can't believe what you're doing. Brian and I are jealous. Are you having a good time?" asked Joni. "Now I know why Bill loves flying. I'm really enjoying the trip. The scenic wilderness is beautiful beyond description. The soft white clouds and the millions of small lakes and rivers go on forever. We've seen a pack of wolves chasing a herd of caribou and also a Grizzly Mom and her two cubs. Bill lowered my wing to look at a moose and I was looking straight down but that doesn't bother me anymore. Tomorrow I'll call you when we get on the ground at Prince George."

"I envy you mom. My boss said he would like to get a plane someday. I told everyone at work what you and Bill are doing."

"Bill says if the weather stays good we'll get there in time for supper," said Gail.

"Please call after you get on the ground in Prince George," asked Joni.

"I will babe, love you, bye."

I lowered the portable cot. "Do you snore?" I asked.

"I don't think so. Do you?"

"Tell me in the morning," I answered.

"I need the bathroom for just a minute, then it's all yours," said Gail. She closed the door and I pulled off my pants and crawled under the covers. I turned on the lamp and got out my Louis L'Amoure western. Gail came out of the bathroom wearing a set of soft pink colored kitty cat pajamas.

"Those are cute pajamas." I said. Idiot, why didn't you bring some pajamas? Maybe she won't notice me in my shorts going to the bathroom, I thought.

"I hope you had as much fun today as I did."

"I'm having a wonderful time," said Gail.

"Are you going to read?" asked Gail.

"For a little while. This is a good Louis L'Amoure western."

"Breakfast is served at 6:00, and I'd like to take off around 7:00 or 7:30. What time do you think we should get up?" I asked.

"Five o'clock, I guess," said Gail.

"Sounds good."

Gail was doing a cross word puzzle and I continued to read my western novel.

"I've only read a few of Louis L'amoure's westerns. I didn't' realize he included steamy sexy scenes in his books. Those cowboys had their pleasures; nothing has changed….our cowboys just have more sophisticated horses now."

A half hour later I said good night and gave Gail a soft kiss. I think I have a little cowboy blood in my veins, I thought, as I turned off the light.

2ND DAY, MORNING, WHITEHORSE

Five o'clock…time to get up, I thought, as I looked over to see if Gail was awake.

"Good morning," said Gail.

"You're already awake," I said.

"I woke up a few minutes ago," said Gail.

The hot shower, loosened up both of our stiff back muscles.

We had our usual breakfast and I limited myself to only one cup of coffee…the three and a half hour non-stop trip was going to be a test of my bladder's endurance. We packed up the two suitcases and headed for the airport. The aviation tower was on our way; we went into the office and filed a flight plan. The weather report indicated clear skies for the next twenty four to thirty six hours. The fuel man was out on the tarmac and I asked him to top off the tanks. I walked around the plane and did the preflight check. Gail waited outside of the plane until the gas man drove away. We climbed into the cockpit and five minutes later we were speeding down the runway, following the highway towards Watson Lake. We passed over the float plane strip and I pointed out the float planes to Gail.

I was excited to be in the air again. Flying in the western Rocky Mountains, a few thousand feet above the terrain was the best seat in the house to view mother nature at her grandest.

The mountains went up steep on my side of the plane and the long broad valley extended below with one long narrow lake after another. The highway was going to be my best choice for an emergency landing if something happened to the airplane. Private airstrips were few and far apart. Forty-five minutes into the flight I angled to the right and started looking ahead for the northern tip of Williston Lake. We said by-by to the Alaska-Canadian highway at this point. For the next three and a half hours we were going to be flying in remote wilderness country. Three thousand feet above the forest allowed me to see over a hundred miles; there was water on the far horizon but it was to early to tell for sure if it was the lake. The compass indicated we were flying south, so l figured the lake would pop up soon.

"There it is; see the body of water up ahead? That's the upper thin arm of Williston Lake. The lake will widen out as we fly further south." Better stay away from the shoreline, I thought.

"The first time I flew this route I followed the shoreline, and the turbulence was bad. It will be a smoother ride if we stay away from the lake." The cold air over the water meeting with the warmer land air creates wind sheer problems, so a wise pilot would choose to fly over either the land or the water for smoother flying.

I told Gail to look for a series of short gravel airstrips every couple of minutes near the shoreline.

"I wonder if I can get Stephannie on the cell phone?" I said.

"I see an airstrip." said Gail, as she laid her head against the head rest and closed her eyes. Her thoughts went back to the Remington. They are probably setting up to play a game of beanbag softball right now.

"Wow! What was that?" asked Gail, as she grabbed hold of my knee. A pencil on the dash floated about a foot in the air as the plane suddenly dropped. The shoulder harness kept us close to the seats, otherwise our heads would of banged into the roof of the cockpit.

"It was a downdraft. We're ok. We're already past it. If we were over by the lake shore we would be getting a lot of bumps." That's what turns your knuckles white," I said, as we both took a deep breath to recover our composure.

2ND DAY 9:30AM, LAKE WILLISTON

"Hello." Stephannie's voice came through loud and clear on the cell phone. Gail pointed at the second airstrip showing two fingers.

"Hi," I said, acknowledging Gail's two fingers.

"Are you flying now?" asked Stephannie.

"We are over the second airstrip on Williston Lake. Everything is, WHOA! I can't talk now, talk to Gail," I said, as I handed the phone to Gail.

"Stephannie, I think the engine just died!" said Gail, with a panic tone in her voice.

I switched the gas tank knob, between the seats, and Gail was getting more panicked by the second.

"We are over the forest near the lake and something is wrong. Bill has lowered the nose of the plane and I think we are in trouble. Pray for us…we are losing altitude…Bill is trying to find out what the problem is. I'm scared… I'll call you soon, if we can solve this problem," said Gail.

Stephannie's world just turned upside down. Dad and Gail were in trouble. The possibility of trouble shocked her mind. I hope they call soon, she thought. Stephannie inhaled a deep breath and looked up at the clock. Fifteen minutes… if they don't call back I'm calling William. She put the portable phone in her pocket and picked up the trash. Her thoughts were totally scrambled. She walked out into the garage and deposited the trash. What if he crashed or landed the plane and had a wreck. Maybe he landed the plane on the airstrip, thought Stephannie.

"Hello, could I speak to William? This is his wife and he needs to come to the phone right away." Wow, that was a clear message, no mixing words, thought the female dispatcher.

"Ok hold on."

"What's up?" William asked.

"Honey, your Dad called fifteen minutes ago and said everything was ok and half a minute later he said there was a problem. Gail took the phone and said she thought the engine had stopped. Dad said something about passing over the second airstrip on Lake Williston. They should of called by now. I have a bad feeling about this. I think they are in trouble."

There was no hesitation on William's part; "I'm coming home right now. I'll be there in a few minutes." William thought about those words, 'I think they are in trouble' and he thought, What can I do? If he crashed he might not have been able to get off an emergency call; no one probably knows that he is in trouble. Alerting the Whitehorse people is all I can do.

"Mike, (William's supervisor), my Dad's flying his plane down from Alaska and he might have had to make an emergency landing. I need to get home and call the Canadian authorities about a possible downed airplane."

"Oh boy, I hope not. Go, family comes first," said William's boss.

As William walked into the living room, he said, "Stef, would you look up on the internet the number for the Whitehorse Tower. I'm going to call them and report a possible downed airplane."

THE CRASH

The seconds were important as I glanced at Gail and squeezed her hand. Stay focused, speak out loud and go through the steps, I thought.

"No engine, switch gas tanks, wait five seconds; pump the throttle, restart the switch. Radio…Mayday, mayday. 52843 engine failure; north end of Williston Lake. Mayday 52843; north end of Williston Lake." There was no reply. Look for landing site, I thought.

Gail was looking outside of the plane, as the plane angled slightly nose down, bringing the forest closer and closer. There's no place to land… we're going to crash, CRASH! The word was echoing in Gail's mind.

No time for shock, I have a job to do, I thought. Gail remained quiet.

Flip the switch on the ELT, look straight ahead at the approaching tree tops, I thought. The propeller was still spinning from the wind, minus the usual hum of the engine.

I looked to make sure Gail had on her seat belt. No openings, I thought as the forest revealed no clear place to land. The hills were a series of ridge lines perpendicular to me and they were blanketed with trees, and the plane had very limited lateral range. A radical turn could drop us instantly. The airspeed of seventy knots was barely enough to keep us from falling like a rock. Every passing second I was losing altitude and I did not want to drop below the level of the next approaching ridge. The landing spot had to be seconds away. We no longer could see the lake. Straight ahead was the only option for a controlled collision. So many pilots in a dead stick emergency try to make a radical turn at the last minute and wind up dropping five hundred feet. I've got to split two trees, and take off the wings, I thought.

A glance at the airspeed indicator showed seventy-five knots. Good, stall near the top of the trees. No slower than sixty-five…The next ridge, gotta do it…. aim for the middle of the trees and then pull up the nose, I thought.

I was zeroed in the direction straight ahead. Be with us now dear God, I thought. Our survival depended on my performance in the next few seconds. Gail said a quick silent prayer as the plane appeared to be heading right into the heart of the forest.

Gail covered her head with her hands as the nearest tree limbs slapped the propeller. We were both thrust forward and the shoulder harness cut into our chests. The trees, that smacked our wings and belly of the plane, gave way as the sixty knot impact had a double effect; the trees swayed upon impact the way a cable works on an aircraft carrier to stop fighter jets from plunging into the sea; the impact ripped away the wings like a brave kid yanking out a loose tooth. The wings were gone in a second and we were thrust forward. The speed of the plane was reduced considerably as we plummeted downward toward the ground. I steered the yoke and pedals to the very end…..my last memory was a satisfying feeling, knowing I had aced the plane exactly between two fir trees.

I learned from other pilots that if one ever had to ditch a plane in a wooded area, with no clearing available, the best scenario is to put the plane between two trees and knock off the wings. The gas tanks on most single engine planes are located in the wings. The gas might explode, but the main body, plus the passengers usually are away from the hot burning fuel.

The wings came off on impact and the airspeed declined instantly. A few seconds after smashing into the trees, Gail opened her eyes and realized that the plane was on the ground and that she survived the crash. The plane was in a nose down position, with the nose touching the ground. The shoulder harness that prevented Gail from impacting the instrument panel was pressing into her chest. The view outside the cockpit window was obscured by the bright green limbs of fir trees about ten feet in front of the plane's propeller.

Gail looked over at me and a second wave of trauma swept over her. He's dead! She thought. I was strapped in by my shoulder harness and my chin was on my chest and my eyes were closed; blood was dripping from my right temple.

"Bill!" Screamed Gail, as she stared at my lifeless looking, limp body. The seconds ticked by as Gail helplessly watched me. Please be alive Bill….Oh God, I need you now, thought Gail.

The wound to my head appeared to be superficial. Gail felt abandoned as she stared out of the cockpit into the silent forest. What am I going to do? I don't know where to start. How will anyone find us? Thought Gail. Gail's mind was working overtime to try and accept the possibility she might be spending the next few days in the forest by herself. She was close to pushing the panic button when she noticed that my chest appeared to be rising and falling. Gail noticed my jaw drop. She could hear that I was breathing. He's alive, she thought. I appeared to be trying to come out of a deep sleep. I moved my head.

"Bill! It's me, Gail…..wake up!"

I touched my head, opened my eyes and looked at Gail. I was slowly trying to understand where I was, and what was happening. I recognized Gail, but confusion reflected in my eyes.

"Bill, we just crashed and you have a nasty bump on your head," said Gail.

I grabbed my seat belt and said, "We need to get out of the plane. Get out!" I yelled, as I unclipped the seat belt and opened my side door.

Gail opened her door and we both stepped out onto the ground. The wheels were knocked off; it was a short step to the ground.

I noticed for the first time that the wings had totally separated from the plane's body. That was good, no fuel, no fire, I thought. As Gail walked around the nose of the plane she never felt any pain. She figured a serious injury would have been apparent right away. I took Gail's hand and said, "Let's sit down." My head was clearing up and I looked at Gail and asked, "Are you ok?"

"I think so," said Gail. We both took a deep breath.

"We need to sit for a while…catch our breath and relax…..We'll know in a little while whether we are hurt or not."

I rubbed my wounded head. The bump had risen considerably over the past few minutes. What hit me? I thought, as I rubbed my head.

Gail's thoughts were all scrambled; Why did I let him talk me into this trip? What if he is seriously hurt internally? What am I going to do? Her anxiety level was snow-balling by the second. She shook her head as she looked at the damaged aircraft.

The plane's wreckage was scattered around, in an area about the size of an average backyard. The trees were tall and thick. The nose of the plane was only about five feet from a wall of thick Fir trees. I'm glad we didn't hit those trees, I thought, looking directly ahead.

"I think I'm ok. Give me a few more minutes. The only thing that hurts is my head… We're lucky to be alive." I could see that Gail was upset and I tried to think of something to say that would give her some comfort.

"We're going to be ok. We have survival gear. We'll stay warm and dry, and there is enough food to last several days."

I moved every joint in my body…..everything seemed to be working normally. Gail was watching my every move. I got the feeling she was praying I was ok. Time was calming my nerves and I was trying to focus on what to do next. Survival was the challenge; all of the camping, fishing and hunting skills I had learned were now going to help us get through this crisis.

I had no words for the moment. The challenge we both faced needed a solution and the shock and awe effect left me at a loss for words. Gail asked me what I was thinking.

"I think I'm a little in shock….This is hard to believe…Everything was so beautiful…you, me, Just moving along so nicely; having a great time and then five minutes later, this…I'm sorry you have to experience this mess." I said, as I reached over and gave Gail a tender hug.

He can think and talk, that's a good sign, thought Gail.

"It's not your fault…What do you think happened?" asked Gail.

"We might of sucked water into the carb and clogged the flow of gas. Sometimes the people who sell gas get water in their tanks and the buyer can get bad gas."

I put my face into my hands and rubbed my eyes.

"Think of this as a three day camping trip…we're going to be fine." I took Gail's hand and gave her a kiss on the cheek.

"I don't remember being asked to go camping," replied Gail, sarcastically.

I thought it best to say nothing. I don't think she wants a reply, I thought.

After, what seemed like an eternity of silence, Gail said, "Look, we've both lost something ….now what do we need to do so I can get back to my family?"

She's right; snap out of it; our lives are more important than our loss, I thought. Gail's spark of tanacity grabbed my attention… Huh…I'm the one that should be encouraging her, I thought.

We both paused and viewed our backyard size of twisted metal. I had never seen the plane without wings. A few bolts anchored the wings to the fuselage and it was easy to see how they could easily be ripped away by some trees.

The plane was in a tight cluster of trees. I thought it would be hard for planes to spot us, and that we would need to move to an open area. I walked over to one of the wings and noticed that the wing tank had not ruptured. The point where the tree impacted the wing was very obvious. The crushed leading edge of the wing was about four feet from the body of the plane. The indentation was a foot wide and about six inches deep.

"The last thing I remember was aligning the plane between two trees."

"The last thing I remember was hearing the limbs smack the plane and thinking we were going to die," said Gail. "We will both probably have flashbacks of seeing the forest swallow us up and slapping the nose of the plane." "I think your right," said Gail.

"You asked what are we going to do…Here's the plan; we're in a tight cluster of trees, It'll be better if we find an open area nearby. The mosquitoes will be bad here, plus smoke will climb better in an open area….We're going to be fine," I said, as I took Gail in my arms and held her tight. "We have each other, it's only going to get better," I whispered into Gail's ear.

"You did a marvelous job of staying calm all the way to the point of impact." "Calm?" Gail looked at me. "Maybe on the outside....I didn't want to distract you."

Talking about the scary incident seemed to help restore a sense of calm and levity. We both took a deep breath as we held each other tight.

"Do we have a first aid kit? You need to have that head wound cleaned up and bandaged," replied Gail.

"Yes. I'll get it. I need something for a splitting headache." The survival gear included medicine and food, plus much more assorted items to make an unexpected camping trip half way comfortable.

Gail cleaned my bloody, swollen temple and said, "You have a nice goose egg. You're as good as new," said Gail.

"I think I'm ok. How about you," I asked Gail, as I stood up and bent slowly down and touched the ground.

"Ok, so far," said Gail, with a face that reflected surprise and spunk. "I'm probably going to have a bruise on my collar bone from the tight shoulder harness. I may also need a smaller size bra if you know what I mean."

"They'll bounce back," I said, with a smile.

The temperature was in the low forties and there was a slight breeze. The sun made the trees and grass shine. I spotted a well packed game trail that passed through our tight cluster of trees. The trail had fresh deer tracks heading further up the ridgeline away from the lake. The trees were too thick to tell if there was some open space.

"Let's go see if we can find an opening. We have a camp to set up, and it won't be long before our appetites are going to kick in."

I led the way, carefully observing the pretty clusters of red fireweed and different varieties of fern plants. The fir tree needles reflected new spring growth. There were bear claw cuts in a few trees, which some say is how the bear mark their territory. One tree trunk was rubbed smooth and shiny, like perhaps a bear took care of a strong itch. Hair was still stuck in some of the bark cracks. About two hundred yards from the wreckage, a pretty meadow was spotted. This is much better, I thought, as I looked at the tall waving grass. The breeze will keep the bugs away. There were some tall cabbage looking plants nearby and I was reminded of similar tall broad leaf plants on the Alaska Peninsula. The up-rooted plants were just like what I saw years earlier. My next thought was BEAR. Only a big powerful bear is capable of up-rooting plants like that. My guess was confirmed seconds later. I spotted a ten inch bear print.

"Look here! Recognize that?" Gail looked at the print. She looked at me and said, "Bear?" "Yep," I said, as we continued walking along the edge of the meadow.

I was reminded of a retired couple who were attacked and killed by a bear in the middle of the night. After being reported overdue, the Alaska State Troopers found body parts and determined that the couple had camped too close to a knoll where there was a cabbage patch clump of weeds. The bear had been feeding on the roots. The best guess, for the attack, was that the couple had invaded a bear's feeding territory; the mistake cost them their lives; although the couple were both well armed, a bear overwhelmed them as they slept in their tent, and they were not able to defend themselves.

We went another quarter mile past the cabbage patch. I better not scare her with that story, I thought.

I was worried about the idea of sleeping in a tent on the ground… We're too close to a known grizzly feeding area. We can't stay here," I thought. I looked at the dense stand of Douglas Fir trees, along the edge of the meadow, and got an idea; a tree platform will work; the trees are close enough to do it; the axe and the rope is all I need to make a good tree platform.

"Ok…..Let's go back and get our gear," I said, feeling better, now that I had what seemed like a good plan.

"Do you think the cell phone might work?" asked Gail

"I never thought of that, it might."

When we got back to the plane I looked all around and eventually found the cell phone under a seat.

"It doesn't work," I said, with a tone of disappointment. "If we were higher up it probably would. I'll turn it off.

The battery will still be good when we get out of here," I said.

I pulled the survival bags out from behind the back seat; there were three bags; food, cooking utensils and gear, such as rope, axe and the 22 rifle. I picked up the two largest bags and let Gail have the lighter bag.

"We're going to get our exercise today," I said, as I turned and headed back to our newly chosen campsite.

"We are really fortunate that neither one of us got a serious injury," I said. That last conversation I had with Stephannie included our location. I hope she remembers and tells William. He knows enough about flying to understand that you call the authorities in a situation like this and tell them what happened…he will make that call and they will find us, I thought.

"How will someone find us?" asked Gail.

"Well….I was just thinking about that. The best thing working in our favor is the cell phone conversation I had with Stephannie. You mentioned we passed over the second airstrip and I told Stephannie that we were over the lake by the second airstrip. If Stephannie or William calls the Whitehorse Tower authorities they will be able to pinpoint our location very accurately. Remember I filed a flight plan this morning back at the Whitehorse tower?" Gail nodded her head. "Well I told them the exact route we were going to fly and all they need to do is follow our route. I said we would close our flight plan when we got to Prince George. I told them a specific time I would call to let them know we were safe and done for the day…..If they don't get that call they will wait thirty more minutes and then start making phone calls; if no one has heard from us an organized search will be initiated and the first day the weather is good the search planes will be out and looking for us. There is another way we can be found…it is more technical but it is effective; that small yellow box, the one I think hit me in the head, it's called an Emergency Locator Beacon. I flipped it on manually just before we crashed; it's suppose to send out a beep, and there are satellites that pick up the signal. A government agency reads those signals and relays the information to the correct nation and within a few minutes Whitehorse knows a distress signal is beeping in their sector. I hope my battery was still good."

"It sounds like the odds are good we will be found soon. Don't you think?" asked Gail.

I looked at Gail, nodded with a smile and said, "Yes. This is going to be a short, simple camping trip." Neither one of us had a clue that this "camping trip" would have more twists and turns than a foot long pretzel.

I didn't bargain for this, Gail thought, as she swatted three mosquitos who were about to suck her blood. Simple camping trip…When does it start? thought Gail. "Do we have any bug dope?" asked Gail.

"Yes. Give me a minute." Gail watched me, searching in the back pack, and thought, Thank you Lord that we didn't get hurt, and thank you that he was prepared for this and knows what to do…she just stared into space at this point.

I was facing a mountain man's ultimate survival test; all of my survival skills were going to come in handy…little did I know the extent of how I was going to be challenged. We've survived a horrendous crash and now it's time to get busy and make the most of a bad situation, I thought. It felt good to be alive.

For Gail, this was like a bad dream, evolving minute by minute… A wonderful trip, down the tubes; reduced to a rough and tumble, primitive camping trip; dirt, mosquitos, sleeping on the hard ground, yuk; the trip had turned into a nightmare within minutes, thought Gail. Gail's imagination could not have exceeded the scope of this evolving nightmare, and how much her knight in shining armor would mean to her before it was all over.

I was thinking about how I would build the tree platform; like Noah and the ark, I was calculating the height, width and length as I walked along the pathway back to the camp.

After I told Gail about my plan to build a tree platform her first thought was a tree platform would be a lot of extra work, plus maybe a little dangerous.

"Why are you going to all that trouble?" asked Gail.

I better not tell her the real truth, I thought.

"You deserve a Penthouse, not just a low budget ground floor tent." "Oh, is that so….it wouldn't have anything to do with a bear?" "Well, maybe a little." He's worried, thought Gail.

She reads my mind like a book, I thought.

Back at the camp I asked Gail if she was hungry.

"A little," was her reply, making no effort to disguise the fact that food was not at the top of her list of concerns. "Ok. Give me a few minutes to get out the goodies."

"Does this bring back memories of your camping days… before you started roughing it in a big plush RV?"

Gail thought for a minute and said, "Yes. I remember a few of those trips, only on this trip we don't have any beverage to soften the bumpy ground."

"Sorry…I'll try to put that in the survival gear next time," I said, with a smile.

She's getting back her sense of humor. Thank you Lord, I thought.

The spaghetti and crackers and V-8 juice hit the spot. It seemed to settle both of our nerves. Not the best…we're not going to starve, I thought.

2ND DAY, NOON AT THE CAMP

Not knowing how long it would take to build the platform, I was anxious to begin the project; it needed to be completed before it got dark.

"Well, I better get busy on the penthouse. I want us to be up there before it gets dark." "Can I do anything to help?" asked Gail.

"I looked around at the dry dead wood and said, "You can gather dry wood and pile it near the fire…that would help." Gail nodded her head.

There were two sixteen inch thick Doug Fir trees, about six feet apart, and I decided to put the platform between them, twenty feet up. Having a project lifted my restless mood….it helped me not to dwell on the obvious loss we were experiencing.

I took my thirty-six inch axe and chopped the limbs, on one side of the trees and left six inch stubs for climbing; this continued until I reached a height of about twenty feet. My biceps got a serious workout climbing and holding onto the tree as I worked my way up. Cramps and pinched nerves would be the price I would pay for this project. My favorite senior phrase was 'You play, you pay'. The second thing to do was cut four inch thick trees for planking. I figured about twenty small trees would do the job. All of the small branches were perfect for a green, smoky fire. The hundred feet of nylon rope, in the survival bag, was perfect for anchoring the planking. After I secured the two cross beams, twenty feet up, Gail slipped the rope onto the small trees, and one by one, the platform came together. Three hours later I tested the six by six platform and it seemed very solid. The project turned out well, and I thought that if my carpenter Daddy were present he would have been impressed.

I put grass and dirt in between the boards to have a smoother surface. It took about another hour to fill the cracks between the boards, plus carry up the tarp, tent and sleeping bags.

Gail was watching the project come together, and she figured the climb to the platform was not going to be easy; she kept herself occupied by keeping the fire blazing hot. I wonder if I can climb up there, thought Gail, as she saw me make several trips carrying dirt and grass and logs.

"I don't know if I can get up there," said Gail.

"Sure you can. I'll give you a boost." This is going to be interesting, I thought, as I followed Gail over to the tree. "Use your feet as much as you can, and your arms won't get so tired."

I followed Gail each step of the way as a confidence booster. She went up slowly and carefully without any trouble.

"Good job," said Gail, admiring the platform and catching her breath. Both of us sat in the penthouse, and took in the view. I was thinking how much more secure a tree platform was going to be. The peace of mind was worth the effort. Sleeping in a tent, on the ground, in the dark, in bear territory would of amounted to a scary long night.

The sky was quickly changing from a shiny blue to patchy gray clouds.

"The weather seems to be changing," I said, looking up above the tree tops. I tied a ridge pole connecting the two large trees about four feet above the platform.

"The tarp will be draped over the pole, so we'll stay dry, if it gets rainy."

The sleeping bags were comfortable. Gail thought they would be warm and comfortable when the time came to snuggle in and get some much needed rest.

"I think I'll take some Aleve before we hit the sack. You should do the same," said Gail.

I nodded my head. "I'm not use to all this physical labor. My arm and shoulder muscles are wasted. I'll be sore tomorrow. I could crawl in the sack right now," I replied. We both sat quietly as we caught our breath. I looked up at the gray clouds that were rolling in and said, "From the beautiful skies, down into the heart of a world where the top of the food chain is often challenged." Gail raised her eye brows with my last comment.

He's thinking the same thing I was thinking, from bliss to yuk in a matter of a few hours, thought Gail. "Yeah, the mosquitos and the bears are not being very respectful," said Gail.

"I'm sure glad you know what you're doing….Do you think your kids know we're in trouble?" Gail asked, as she rested, leaning back against the smooth white trunk of the fir tree.

I looked at Gail and pondered her question. "Yes. Stephannie probably called William and told him about our phone conversation. William or Stephannie will call Myndi, Sonnet, and Lilly as soon as they find out we are missing. My girls will get in touch with their mother; William will call your family…..by night fall our families will be worried sick trying to get through this crisis…William is familiar with flying procedures and flight plans; my guess is he'll call Whitehorse and notify them of our situation. I hope Stephannie remembers the part about the lake and the second airstrip."

WILLIAM REPORTS A POSSIBLE ACCIDENT

"Hello, Whitehorse Aviation Office, how may I help you?"

"I am calling from Prince George, B.C.. My Dad and his girl friend left from the Whitehorse Airport this morning in a Cessna 172. Can you confirm this for me?" asked William.

"What was his name sir?" replied the airport official.

"Bill Parker."

"We have a flight plan…two people; they left 07:30; Whitehorse to Prince George via the Trench."

"Ok, well, here's the situation. My Dad called about 9:30 this morning and talked about a minute on a cell phone, and then he said he had a problem. An hour has gone by and we have not heard from them. My Dad told my wife he was near Lake Williston, above the second airstrip."

"Lake Williston has a series of airstrips on the northern end, about five minutes apart. My guess is your Dad was counting the airstrips as he was flying south…..just a minute please. I'm going to switch you to my supervisor."

"Hello Hal Wilcox."

"Hello, I'm William Parker. Did you get the information about my Dad, Bill Parker?"

"Yes I did. I'm glad you called. Your cell phone conversation might help us if we need to conduct a search. Your Dad's flight was a three and a half hour trip to Prince George. We officially make phone calls starting thirty minutes after a flight plan has expired; that will be about three hours from now. We will red flag this situation and contact you this evening before I leave the office….Give us a call if your Dad contacts you."

"Ok. I'll be standing by for your call," answered William, with an apprehensive tone in his voice. William told Stephannie they would be getting a call from the Whitehorse people later in the evening. The rest of the afternoon William and Stephannie hung out near the phone just in case Dad's call came through. The hours went by slowly.

WHITEHORSE, AVIATION PEOPLE

"Hello," answered Fred Summers, a dentist in Whitehorse. "Hello, Hal Wilcox here. We have a rescue mission for tomorrow, if the weather cooperates. I need you to line up as many pilots as you can. The target area is the Trench, at the north end of Lake Williston; ask everyone to be on stand-by status for an 8:00 o'clock take-off at the Watson Lake airstrip." Like a volunteer fireman, Fred committed his flying skills for search and rescue operations; his dental appointments took a back seat when it came to searching for downed aircraft.

"Hello," answered William.

"Hal Wilcox. Your Dad has not closed his flight plan, so weather permitting, in the morning our Civil Air Patrol team will be looking for his aircraft. I'm hoping we find your Dad and his passenger safe and sound on one of those gravel airstrips. Their cell phones will not work on the ground in that area."

"I hope so too. We'll be sitting by the phone," William replied.

"A storm is coming up from the south. We might be able to get into the area in the morning. I will keep you posted."

"Thank you; we're not going anywhere," answered William.

William looked at his watch and figured, they would be getting into Prince George right about now, if everything had gone according to plan…He didn't mention anything about an ELT alert. I hope they didn't go down in the lake, thought William. The emotional upheaval that occurs in situations like this, were fast impacting William's nerves.

2ND DAY 4:00PM, TREE PLATFORM FINISHED

"I'm sorry I got you into this mess," I said, as I gave Gail a sad look; like the kicker who missed the potential game winning field goal.

Gail sensed that the events of the past few hours had taken a heavy toll on my morale; the injury, and loss of the plane was a hard pill to swallow.

"We're both alive...We can be thankful for that." Gail was trying to be positive. It was unsettling for her to see me look so forlorn.

I looked at Gail and thought, Snap out of it...a self-pity trip is not going to help, I thought. You didn't do anything wrong...You did what you were trained to do to survive; She's right, what's done is done... we still have our health and future....that's what I need to focus on.

"Back at the restaurant you said you were glad I brought you on this trip...do you still feel that way?" I said.

Gail searched for the right words, and then said, "After we get back home and get cleaned and rested up I'll probably say something like, 'The inconvenience we went through was minor compared to the good times we've shared.' Does that make any sense?" asked Gail.

Gail's smile and words warmed my heart and soul. Her presence at that moment must have been what a flower experiences when the drought is followed by a soothing rain.

"You ought to give writing a go....That was a beautiful thought... thank you," I said.

"Shall we get down? We need to go get some water," I replied.

"We're getting our exercise today," said Gail, as she followed her man down the tree.

"I'll sleep well tonight," said Gail.

"It's good I'm going down first; I'll break your fall if you slip."

"Ha, Ha. I'm not going to give you that satisfaction," laughed Gail. We headed down the game trail towards the plane.

When I walked up to the pilot side of the airplane I noticed the seats were shredded and that suit cases had been ripped open; clothes were scattered all over, and the plastic water bottles were punctured; the water had leaked out. Stay calm, I thought to myself. Don't upset her.

"We've had a visitor. A bear probably smelled something in the suit cases. Our water is gone. Look at the seats." Holy cow! It's a pretty bold bear. I'm going to get the compound bow, I thought.

"I'm going to take my bow and arrows. It looks like one bottle still has some water," I said, as I surveyed the back seat of the plane. Fear prompted me to quickly get the compound bow and string an arrow and head back to camp. I felt about as safe as a sparrow in a hawks nest.

"Ok, let's get out of here," I said, with an obvious anxious tone of concern about our safety.

As we walked back to camp my eyes now took on that radar look that I had talked to Gail about, back in the lodge cafe. Broad daylight….. that's unusual for a bear……that tree platform idea sounds a lot better now, I thought.

We walked down the trail in silence. I know this can kill a bear, I thought, as I looked at the bow, but, how quickly, and where do I aim? If we are attacked in the trees can the bear get to the platform? What happens if he gets to the platform? What do we do at that point? Concern about our security brought up a long list of questions that completely caused me to forget my tired aching muscles.

"We'd be wise to keep our eyes open and not to walk into the trees alone," I said, as I scanned the forest up ahead.

"Do you think a grizzly can climb up to our platform?" asked Gail.

"I don't know…..I'd guess no, but I'm not sure."

"Have you ever killed anything with that bow?"

"No, but I've seen hunters do it on T.V. This thing is a powerful weapon and it can kill a bear or moose, if I hit it in the right place. I bought it for moose hunting, but I've never had a chance to take it on a hunting trip."

Gail was thinking; Ok let me fill in the blanks; we don't know if we're safe in the trees; he hasn't killed a large game animal, but he has seen others do it…I think I have reasons to be nervous. We both had a lot to think about as we headed for the camp. I looked at the compound bow and thought, I better sharpen those broad-heads….It might be a good idea to set the pin from twenty yards down to ten yards and take some practice shots.

"That's pretty good shooting," said Gail, as she watched me taking a few practice shots.

"It'll do. If I must take a shot, I'm going to aim for the gut. It's guaranteed to do a lot of damage."

"Have you ever seen a grizzly at the zoo or in a movie?" I asked.

"In a movie," answered Gail.

"They are tall when they stand up. A mature grizzly's head would be about half way up to our platform if it stood up."

The more I thought about the bear that tore up the seats, the more worried I got. If it does that in broad daylight what will it do when it gets dark? Is it better to be quiet or should I tell her about my concern?

"I've got to be honest….I'm worried; the bear that ripped up the plane seats is probably the same bear that rooted up the plants. We are trespassing in his backyard. I think there's a good chance we might be visited by this bear tonight……We need to get prepared for a possible attack." I looked into Gail's eyes to see how this last comment registered. Gail gave me a sober stare that implied you have my attention, actually you have me scared….now what do we do?

"I have a few ideas that might help us stay alive."

ALIVE…This word jolted Gail's consciousness, similar to someone touching a poorly grounded refrigerator. "See the two trees above the platform? I'm going to cut the branches above the platform so we can climb higher, in case the bear reaches the platform. When, or if I tell you to climb, you must go immediately……no hesitation. It won't be easy in the dark. You're a brave girl, when you have to be, and I know you can do this. If a bear comes around I will try to scare it away, but if it doesn't run, and attacks, I'll shoot and try to kill it."

I looked into Gail's eyes to see if she was grasping my instructions; she could not have possibly appeared more focused. "That's the plan... You understand your part?"

Gail looked into my eyes and nodded her head.

"You think we might be attacked tonight?" asked Gail.

My response was slow in coming.......Yes."

"We won't be the first to be attacked by a grizzly at night, if it happens. A few years ago, in Alaska, a couple, our age, were sleeping in their tent, and in the middle of the night, a grizzly attacked and killed them both......we will have a better chance than they did. The tree platform gives us a chance to fight back. A big bear can growl loud and this can be scary. My advice is just stick out your tongue, like you would at a bully by the Principal's office, and blow your lips...remember you have an escape route....and, well, I'll do whatever needs to be done."

And that's suppose to give me a lot of comfort? thought Gail.

I was trying to cover all the bases. "One more point; if something happens to me, here's something you need to know....and do. Good weather and a smoky fire is our ticket out of here. The first day the weather is good there will be planes up in the air looking for us; about two hours after the sun comes up we need to have smoke going up into the sky to attract the planes; remember this, and you will be ok." To bad I wasn't this thorough making sure the plane was properly fueled and serviced, I thought.

I looked at Gail and saw fear in her eyes, and I finished up the discussion with, "We are prepared for the worst... we've just got to be patient and make good decisions while we wait to be rescued."

Gail thought, I hope there's no bears tonight.

"Let's get a big fire going," I said, as I threw more kindling onto the fire. I felt that there were eyes nearby watching our every move.

I glanced at my watch; my anxiety level seemed to increase with every passing minute as we stood by the fire. It would be seven o'clock by the time we finished dinner; that was ok. I figured to tie-up the food after dinner and then climb onto the platform and rest for the next twelve hours.

The sky was totally over cast. The gray clouds had moved in quickly. The dinner consisted of crackers, cheese, Tuna and V8 juice. Not in the mood for small talk, very little was discussed while we feasted by the warm, crackling fire.

"We may get rain tonight." If it rains, I thought, the night sounds will be muffled and it will be easier for a grizzly to walk into our camp undetected.

I pulled the food pack up beyond the reach of any and all four legged critters.

"Let's get up on the platform." Gail went over and climbed up the tree like she had been doing it all her life; I went up right behind her.

I chopped off the branches on both trees so we could climb higher if necessary; Gail decided to crawl into her sleeping bag.

That should do it, I thought, as I sized up the extra ten feet of climbing space. Fatigue was starting to kick in and it was a relief to lie down on the sleeping bag. I closed my eyes to rest for a few minutes. I could hear Gail snoring. It's been a hard day for both of us, I thought. Our lofty perch was a comfortable blessing…it not only put us high above the ground, but it also elevated our security level.

Am I over-reacting? All this worry about a bear.…. My mind was seeing the situation clearly; evidence indicates bear activity.…in the bright of day. Usually bears are most active in the latter hours of the day and night. The bear might be old or crippled and not able to forage for food. Going into the plane in broad day light was a sign of boldness, or desperation. All of this second guessing was going on in my mind, and slowly, but surely, like an incoming tide, sleep was trying to get the upper hand.

Half in the warm bag and half out, with my back resting against the tree, I thought, Dear Father in Heaven be with us tonight; be with our kids…help us get through this storm; give us strength and wisdom; thank you for the miracle today; thank you for your mercy, grace and your peace right now…In Jesus's name.

The bow and arrows were hung within easy arms reach, as well as a staff about eight feet long, with a sharp pointed tip.….one more weapon to discourage an angry bear.

WILLIAM'S HOME, PRINCE GEORGE

Stephannie went out for some local fast food for dinner. Dad's been preparing for something like this all of his life.

He'll be ok if he didn't get hurt, thought William.

William stared at the carpet from his recliner. The cloud of concern was churning away in his gut and mind.

Anxiety had the juices going and sleep was not going to come easy.

"Do we have a sleeping sedative? I'm not going to get any sleep otherwise?" "How about a glass of wine?" asked Stephannie. "We have some?"

"There's that bottle that we got when we exchanged gifts at Christmas." "Ok, I'll pop the cork; I hope we get some news soon," said William.

2ND DAY EVENING IN PRINCE GEORGE

"Hello Mr. Parker. This is Hal Wilcox, from Whitehorse. I called to inform you that no one has heard from your Dad. I have a crew of pilots ready to go. Our planes will be out at the first opportunity; tomorrow is kind of iffy, because of a storm. The storms usually come and pass within 24-48 hours. I'll call you as soon as we have some news to report."

"We'll be waiting for your call," said William. Whew, thought William, as the latest grim news about Dad suddenly began to weigh heavier on his mind.

"That was a Whitehorse official. They haven't heard from Dad…all we can do is wait until they have some news to give us. The weather is getting bad and they might not be able to fly tomorrow. I better make a few calls…..including Gail's daughter. She is probably expecting a call this evening. I'm glad Dad gave us her number." Where's that wine? Thought William.

2ND DAY 9:00PM ON THE PLATFORM

The wind woke me from a sound sleep. The temperature had dropped within the past hour. Rain seemed imminent. A storm was definitely brewing. The tree tops were swaying back and forth. This jeopardizes our chances of getting out of here tomorrow; that's ok. We'll take it one day at a time, I thought.

The nap lifted my spirits. The short rest seemed to improve my attitude regarding our circumstances. I was feeling more like, ok we've suffered a setback, but things are going to get better with each passing day. If we're stuck here tomorrow we'll need to go find some water….. we'll need to walk off this ridge and go down hill, I thought.

Like an inmate, in a prison cell, there was no place I could go, and nothing to do, except try to stay calm, alert and positive.

"You've gotta walk that lonesome valley…You've gotta walk it by yourself….Nobody else can walk it for you"; the words of this song popped into my head. I was reminded of the time when the doctor told me the squamous skin cancer had spread to my lymph gland, below the jaw. The cloud of anxiety, wondering if the cancer had spread to other parts of my body, was another one of those cannot control and did not cause storms of life….like taxes, they never go away………neither do you, Lord, I thought.

The dark, gray clouds cast a semi- darkness upon the forest, even though we had a few more minutes before darkness set in. I could see the fire clearly, about fifteen yards away.

The trees, with their shadowy areas, were difficult to see through; anything could lurk there and be well concealed.

THE BEAR ATTACK 2ND DAY 9:30PM CAMP

What's that? I thought, as I bolted into a straight back sitting position; a clear, for sure snapping of a branch.

Maybe a deer.....It's time for deer to start feeding. I held my breath, listening for another sound. I didn't have long to wait. My worst fear appeared out of the trees; it was a full grown, massive grizzly…Wow, let Gail sleep; maybe it will move on, I thought. The bear sniffed around the fire. The bear was below the back pack. It must of detected a scent coming from the pack. It stood up on its hind legs and reached, but the food was about five feed beyond its reach. The bear circled the fire with nose to the ground. It seemed to be following another scent; it turned in the direction of the platform. This is not good, I thought. The animal appeared to be following our scent. Go. Get out of here, I thought to myself. The bear was on all fours, and he was using his large bulging nose the way a trained dog would search for a particular smell. It took about thirty seconds for the bear to travel the forty feet to the tree trunk below me. The beast reared up and came to its full height; I estimated it to be eight or nine feet tall. My organs were responding to the adrenaline that was spreading to every muscle cell in my body. The over-riding question was will it give up and wander away. My thoughts were, Stay calm….Don't move. The bear registered a scent that would soon culminate into an encounter that neither man nor beast could have predicted.

I figured I could scare the bear away with a strong loud yell, but I didn't want to yell and alarm Gail. The bear, did not follow Smokey's

Rules of Bear Etiquette. The beast's massive nostrils were pulsating to help locate the source of the faint scent. The small red eyes locked onto me looking down at him. The bear let out a snort, which was probably the equivalent of "Gotcha!" in bear talk. The bear started smacking his jaws and let out a growl; it was clear the bear had made his choice for dinner. Time to see if yelling will scare him off, I thought.

"Get out of here!" Three things happened almost simultaneously; I yelled; Gail jumped, sat up and screamed, and the bear let out a defiant roar. My first thought was, the bear is not leaving, and its now time for action; I swung to get the bow and arrows and yelled, "Climb up the tree, NOW!" Gail didn't hesitate. She headed up the tree like a trained Navy Seal.

This frightening event reminded Gail of the dog attack when she was a seven year old child. Three big neighborhood dogs ran up to her and knocked her down. She was in her front yard and she screamed as the dogs approached her. Her big brother scared the dogs away before they could inflict major damage. The trauma of that moment stayed in her memory, and now, once again, a similar incident was happening. The sight of the huge teeth and the thunderous growl sent an electrifying shock throughout her entire body; from a sound sleep to a trauma drama. "FLIGHT" was the message she received, and with the adrenaline boost, going up the tree was no problem. The light of the evening shadows was plenty clear for finding the hand and foot holds for getting up higher into the tree. She gripped the branches with white knuckles and a red flushed face; her fear was not reduced by climbing higher. The bear was not going away; drastic action was the only way to try and discourage the aggressive attack; living to see another sun rise depended on my hunting skill with a bow and arrow.

The bear, standing at full length, circled the tree we used to climb up onto the platform. It was methodically planning the best way to get to us.. The massive claws were only about eight feet away from the platform. The bear went under the platform. I couldn't get a shot. The bear acted like it was going to attempt to climb one of the trees. I could hear a crunching sound; the bear was chewing limbs so it could wrap its massive body around the tree trunk. No fear; this animal acts like its been eating people all its life, I thought, as I decided to grab the sharp spear to see if I could slow down the aggressive attack. Try to take out one of the eyes, I thought. The bear slapped at the spear and would not allow the stick to come near its face.

Gail was as high as she could go in the tree. She could only pray at this point. I got on my belly trying to distract and discourage the animal; the beast was not backing away.

It appeared to be coming down to who had the best weapons. I couldn't out muscle the bear; I had to use my wits. What could I do? The spear, at best, was only a small distraction. I need a clear shot; maybe if I throw something it will pursue and give me a shot. This pole is, at best, just a stand-off. Thank God it can't climb a tree like a black bear, I thought. It all felt so unreal. The stand-off, I felt, was only temporary. The bear didn't act a bit afraid of my puny weapon.

I felt a calmness, even though a ferocious killer was only eight feet away. I knew the animal was capable of pulling my body apart, like plucking zucchini off of the vine. It seemed only a matter of time before the bear chewed a clear path up to the platform. The powerful jaw teeth chewed away a limb about every thirty seconds. This nonsense has gotta stop. Maybe if I take off my shirt and throw it towards the fire? Got to give it a try, I thought. I took off my shirt and yelled, "Go get it!" as I threw the shirt down and towards the fire.

The bear took the bait. I quickly grabbed the bow and arrow. The bear charged over and grabbed the shirt with its teeth and proceeded to shake its head back and forth. The shot was there, as the animal's back was exposed. I drew the arrow and launched a shot that penetrated the right rear portion of the dark red twisted hairy beast. Three-fourths of the shaft penetrated into the animals body; this one shot alone would eventually cause the animal to bleed to death…When, was the question?

The bear spun around trying to find what had inflicted the pain in its back. The beast glanced up at the platform, as if to see if his prey was still there, and then it lumbered back over and resumed the task of chewing away at the limbs. I thought, Now we're back with the same problem. It worked once, maybe it'll work again? I emptied my pockets and took my pants off and threw them down to the ground. The bear didn't go for it this time. I took a deep breath and pondered what to do next. I thought, I can't shoot because the platform is in the way......I've got to get some more shots, so what can I do? I looked at the small six foot long cross pieces of the platform and the rope I used to bind the pieces together. I thought, If I cut the rope I can spread a few of those poles and maybe get a good shot straight down. The first pole came away quickly as did the other four or five poles. This might work, I thought, as I began to create an opening to launch a few more shots.

The massive skull would probably deflect a broad-head arrow, so I aimed for a spot that would be considered the clavicle area on a human being.....maybe I could take out a lung....hopefully. The arrow penetrated into the fur and disappeared. The animal hesitated and then went back to chewing only at a much slower pace. I quickly strung another arrow and aimed for the opposite shoulder; the arrow likewise penetrated and disappeared into the huge body cavity; The third shot sent the bear into a frenzy of confusion...it went to all fours and remained motionless. I quickly strung a fourth arrow and aimed at the base of the skull; This arrow also penetrated the hide and disappeared from sight......How much is it going to take to kill this thing, I thought, as the bear lumbered towards the fire.

Time stood still, it seemed, as I watched the bear slowly retreating for the first time since the battle began. Keep going, I thought, as the bear slowly disappeared into the dark shadows of the forest. A few seconds went by, after the bear left, when I glanced up at Gail clinging to the tree limbs. The silence was a reminder to breathe again, as I looked up and said, "Come on down."

Gail's muscles trembled and felt extremely weak. The gray daylight was going fast. I suspected Gail's nerves were extremely frayed. We both sat down and I held Gail in my arms and stroked her hair. Her arms were cold and trembling. Tears started to roll down her cheeks. She inhaled deeply and expanded her chest.

"I didn't bargain for this," said Gail, as she pressed her cheek against my shoulder.

Little did I realize the trauma that was now imbedded in Gail's sub-conscious mind.

"Crawl into the bag. I'll stay awake and keep watch," I said.

Sitting next to Gail I felt a weakness in my joints. The situation reminded me of the time a hurricane force storm prevented my wife from flying to the hospital when she went into labor. The only way to get to the hospital was by flying in a small plane. I delivered my own son in our small fishing cabin. The delivery went fine and the village nurse arrived in time to clean up and cut our son's umbilical cord. I handled the stress ok until I stepped out the front door into the fresh air; my whole body felt weak.

I massaged Gail's neck and shoulder muscles; she was extremely tense; we both could have benefited by a couple of shots of brandy.

We would both be dead now if we had been on the ground, I thought, as I retied the platform boards.

"Uh oh." The rain started falling. I grabbed the tarp and flapped it over the log above the platform.

"The bear will probably be dead before the sun comes up. The worst is behind us... We're safe up here." Gail took a deep breath and seemed to have gotten her second wind. "You going to stay awake?" Gail asked.

"Yes. Go ahead and try to get some sleep."

"Are you ok?" asked Gail.

"I'm fine."

"I don't think I'll be able to get any sleep," said Gail, as she crawled into her bag.

After a few minutes I could hear Gail's heavy breathing. It's going to be a long night, I thought. Darkness had finally come and all I could hear was the light patter of rain drops on the tarp. Let's see if this frog light works, I thought. The flashlight was fully charged. There was smoke coming up from the camp fire and no four legged critters.

De ja vue, I thought. I was reminded of the time when I was about sixteen years old. Dad and I and two uncles were on our annual, opening weekend, deer hunting trip. I took my sleeping bag, rifle and flash light and walked about a half mile from the camp ground. The plan was to sleep on the ground and wake up thirty minutes before daylight and catch a deer fleeing the first wave of hunters fanning out into the woods. It was a good plan, with one exception......I didn't anticipate the critters that surrounded me all night. My flash light revealed little green eyes glowing in the dark shadows of the pine and fir trees. I was taught that the California Sierra Nevada Mountain animals might be a nuisance, but not a threat; my instincts were telling me something different. My instincts told me this was a dumb idea. The sleeping bag was not deep enough. I kept telling myself that the forest animals were more afraid of me than I was of them; it was a long night.

The rain, hitting the plastic tarp, drowned out any chance of hearing the night sounds. Fatigue eventually overtook me and I nodded off into a deep sleep. The need to urinate during the night was the only thing that interrupted a good sound sleep.

A new day greeted us with a gray cloud layer, only five hundred feet above the tree tops. With the new day, also came a fresh new wave of optimism—being rescued.

3ᴿᴅ DAY DAWN CAMP

I stood up and relieved myself. With no pants and cold legs, I watched the trickle of fluid descend twenty feet to the ground. I recalled my cousin saying, (as a child), that I had chased some of the kids down the alley threatening to pee on them. Family reunions have a way of bringing back one's sordid past life. No planes today, probably. That's ok, after last night things will only get better, I thought.

I tip-toed gently, so as not to awaken Gail, and climbed down to the ground. With my spear for protection, I looked into the trees as far as possible for any sign of a bear......nothing. The ground was wet. The fire was completely extinguished. I retrieved my wet pants and shredded wet shirt. My body was starting to shake from the cold. I figured wearing wet clothes was better than standing around in my shorts. Starting a fire was the first thing on my mind. As I trembled all over, I gathered the small dry branches from Gail's pile of wood. I proceeded to snap, crack and compress the wood. My pocket bic fire starter ignited into a flame about thirty seconds later. I slowly placed larger branches on the pile. The damp ground and my half chilled body did not sit very well with my spoiled Remington lifestyle. The heat felt good on my belly as I pulled out my shirt to get some of the rising heat. I dropped the food pack from the tree and retrieved some food. I'm glad it's not raining, we've got to go get some water, I thought.

"Hey!" said Gail, as she crawled out of the sleeping bag. "Having breakfast without me?" "Come on down. It's safe," I said.

"How do you feel?" I asked, as Gail walked over by the fire, rubbing the bark off her hands.

"I could use a hug." Gail said. It felt good when I took off my wet shirt and embraced Gail. Women seem to know, better than us men, what's good for the soul.

"Did the bear shred your shirt?" asked Gail.

"Yep. It was one small step for the bear and one good shot for me," I said, with a smile.

"Did that bed agree with your body?" I asked, as I held my shirt over the fire.

"Oh, it was marvelous. I have sore muscles I didn't know existed," said Gail. "That's right. You threw your clothes on the ground last night," said Gail, as she noticed my pants were also wet. "That was a clever idea. I saw the first arrow hit the bear in the back. That was better than watching a home run shot go into to the brink at Candlestick Park," said Gail. I beamed with pride after that compliment, and put my best foot forward by keeping my mouth shut, like, Oh, it was no big thing.

"I'm hungry, cold and I've got to go pee." said Gail.

"Gotcha. Go that way and don't go far. The bear went that way," I said, pointing in the opposite direction. When Gail got back from her nature call she asked, "Is the bear problem behind us?"

"I put four arrows in that thing….. It's in bear heaven."

Gail looked at me and shook her head.

"Peaches ok?" She asked.

"Thank you."

As Gail went through the food pack, picking crackers and peanut butter to round out her breakfast, she asked, "Do you think you could make us some furniture….something to sit on by the fire?"

"That's a good idea…I should be able to come up with something." I figured three logs would do the trick; after scouting the nearby woods I found some dead tree trunks. I was able to flatten one side and it made a perfectly good clean seat. After finishing the job, I thought, I just did my first "honey-do" project.

As I gazed into the fire I thought, she's awful quiet; I hope she's gotten over the shock of last night.

"Are you ok?" I asked.

Gail looked into my eyes...after a few seconds of struggling with her thoughts, she said, "That was a night from hell. I've never experienced anything that scary in all of my life.... I thought we were going to be killed...Twice, in twenty-four hours." Gail shook her head and looked to see if her words were understood.

I looked at Gail and the pain I saw made my eyes water—all I could do was nod my head.

"I'm glad I built that platform...probably one of the wisest decisions I've ever made."

"I felt alone and abandoned after the plane crash....I thought you were dead for a while there....I was angry at myself for letting you talk me into this trip," said Gail.

I was stung by her last comment. I thought, Is our relationship unraveling?

"I don't feel that way now...You didn't cause us to be in this predicament, and I know in a few more days life will return to normal....I'm afraid to think about tonight and what might happen; can you understand?"

At this point Gail's emotion got the best of her and the tears began to flood her eyes. I put my arms around her trembling shoulders.

Bear attacks are rare, but she's afraid we are going to be attacked again tonight, I thought.

"I can't promise, but the odds of being attacked again by another bear tonight is highly unlikely. The nature of a bear is to avoid people. Bear attacks are rare and we are safe up on the platform. The odds of being attacked two nights in a row would be like getting struck by lightening two days in a row. Does that give you a little peace?"

"I can't erase the memory of last night," said Gail.

"We'll both probably have nightmares about last night for a long time; we're going to be fine. We'll get up on the platform before dark and we'll be safe up there."

3RD DAY 8:30AM CAMP

After a belly full of breakfast I finished drying and thoroughly saturating my clothes with wood smoke.

"Are you up for a hike? I asked Gail. Gail gave me a 'What's up?' look. "We need water, and I'm guessing we'll find it down in that canyon."

"Do you think I would let you go and leave me here? I'm your shadow until we get out of these woods," said Gail in a tone of voice that made it perfectly clear that wherever I went, she was sure to go. I Thought, Will she still want me around after we get out of the woods?

"Ok, we can take the rain ponchos in case it starts raining; if you carry the spear, I'll carry the bow," I said, as I hooked the water bottle to my belt. I said a quick silent prayer, Be with us today dear God…In Jesus's name. I'm not a deeply religious person, but God knows I revere Him and value His wisdom and guidance. Some days, I get busy and forget to pray.

I led the way following a game trail. The safest way down into the canyon was on an angle, slowly going down hill. The downward angle of the game trail was easy walking. The forest reminded me of the beautiful California Sierra Mountains. Birds were fluttering from tree to tree ahead of us. There were fallen tree trunks we either climbed over or walked around. There was plenty of red spongy looking snow plants that glowed with a fresh layer of moist water. Every hundred yards, or so, I used tree limbs to point the way back to camp. There were fresh deer tracks everywhere. An occasional tree had bear claw marks about eight feet high and there was lots of bear scat and deer droppings littering the trail.

About thirty minutes into the hike we could faintly hear the noise of a creek up ahead. We came to a small trickle of a stream that had popped out of the earth somewhere higher up on the mountain. The small stream cut across our trail.

"Lots of deer track here," I said, as I stopped where the water crossed the trail.

That looks like a pile of tailings from someone who's been panning gold, I thought, as we paused by the creek. There was a small mound of dirt and rock along the side of the stream. We continued on down the trail and expected to intercept a large creek that we could hear, possibly around the next bend.

"What's that?" I said, as I spotted a small wooden structure further down the trail.

"What do we have here?" The structure was a small cabin with a good solid looking roof and strong six inch pine beam walls; it was only about twelve feet square. I walked entirely around the cabin and didn't find a door.

"That's odd…no door…I bet there's an entrance in the ground…. maybe like the way the ancient far north people built their igloos. This might have been a trapper cabin built by the Indians."

I took the spear, and poked in the ground along side of each wall. As I walked around the first two walls I found only soft dirt. The dirt along the third wall produced a hallow thud. The soil was very loose and there was no layer of debris; just typical loose dark soil. About two inches into the dirt I uncovered a man-hole type cover made out of two by six lumber. I lifted the three foot square cover and there was a hole that went down about four feet. This is the door, I thought. It's a pretty clever idea…..it would discourage a bear. The hole straddled the foundation of the outside wall. I had room to drop into the hole and by bending my knees I was able to move past the bottom log and stand up inside the cabin. A bear would have a very difficult time trying to squeeze through the opening, I thought.

"I hope there's no dead body inside," I said, as I disappeared from sight and left a nervous Gail standing outside all alone and vulnerable.

"Come on in!" While my eyes were nearly adjusted to the dim light, Gail was not yet aware of the contents of the cabin. I went to about a dozen holes in the cabin wall and pulled out cloth and pine needle stuffing from each hole. The light clearly revealed a table, bed and boxes. There was a lantern on the table, with half a tank of fuel.

"I was hoping we would find a microwave and a big flat screen TV." said Gail.

"Ha, Ha," I said.

"I'll try to get this lantern lit," I said. After a few compressions I turned the lever and heard the fine spray of fuel. I put the match inside the glass and instantly the filaments took on a steady increasing glow; the cabin's interior was well lit.

"There's no stove." I thought it strange, a cabin with no stove.

Gail asked if the metal five gallon can, over by the wall, could be a stove. The can was on the ground about a foot from the wall. I walked over and looked at the can and noticed there was a hole about three inches in diameter near the top.

"You're right. I see a vent pipe that goes from the can into the wall. Pretty primitive stove, but sometimes you make do until something better comes along."

There were boxes at the end of the bed which contained can goods. The wool bedding was fresh looking.

"Someone's been here recently.....these blankets are dust free," I said, as I sat on the bed.

"Maybe we better get out of here. Someone may show up any moment," I said.

Gail was comforted by the fact that we had discovered a shelter, but she agreed…they were trespassing. "Yeah, good idea… Goldilocks, I am not."

We put the plugs back in the holes; turned out the light and awkwardly went back out the entrance of the cabin and replaced the wooden door.

"There, just the way we found it; let's check out the area." I said.

The small stream that crossed the trail wound its way within ten yards of the cabin; this stream merged into a large fast moving stream about forty yards down the hill. I led the way in the direction of the small creek.

We both spotted an object that was disturbing and puzzling. We walked over to a large brown boot with a bloody splintered object protruding out of the boot.

"Yuk!" said Gail, as she squeamishly turned her head. The object was all that remained of a human leg. The skin and tendons surrounded the long bone fragment. Dried blood, flies and small bees were feasting on the protein rich delicacy. My first thought was we were looking at the remains of a bear attack victim; the person tried to kick and discourage the attacker, and in the process, one big bite and the lower foot was totally severed.

The sight sent a shock wave through my mind and throughout my body. My senses became heightened…I quickly spanned the entire area for more clues that might explain the tragic event that had unfolded recently. The flesh, bone and blood protruding out of the boot seemed surreal…it was all that remained of a human being. Just a piece of meat to another animal but the human race processes the viewing of bloody dismembered body parts differently.

"Let's sit down. That's a man's foot!"

No shit Sherlock, thought Gail.

"It's not very old," said Gail

"I wonder where the rest of the body is?" I said, as I looked around.

"The sight of blood never bothered me much, but this makes me want to vomit," said Gail.

"Yeah, when I saw body parts from a road mine explosion in Vietnam I nearly puked"

I reached out and gave Gail a hug.

"Not to make light of the subject, but did you see Jurassic Park?" I asked.

"Yes." Those prehistoric creatures were eating and scattering body parts all over the place…. aren't we lucky…. we get to see the real stuff," commented Gail, as she gave me a disgusted look.

"I don't think there is anything funny about this whole scene." We both stared in silence as we shook our heads trying to wrap our minds around the horror that must have occurred in the not to distant past. He must of really fought hard to get his leg free, I thought.

"Look at that!" I said. Gail followed my line of sight and saw what I got excited about; there was a rifle leaning up against a tree; I walked over and examined the rifle; it was a slightly rusted 30.06, bolt action rifle; there was a bullet in the chamber and four shells in the magazine. Thank you Lord for this gun, I thought.

I noticed a few feet from the rifle that there mounds of familiar black dirt. Is that gold dirt? I thought. I noticed the little creek, only a few feet away, had small logs placed crosswise in the stream about a foot apart. A primitive sluice box…that's a clever idea, I thought.

I explained to Gail that I suspected the victim was probably a gold prospector. I pointed out the rich, black sand and the primitive sluice box. Gail noticed a shovel on the other side of the creek. I looked around the area for a gold pan, but no such luck. Maybe it was washed away by the current, I thought.

"I have an idea." I took a water container and scooped up some dirt on the high-side of one of the logs in the stream. I swished the dirt and water, and in less than a minute the glitter of shiny gold appeared; what I saw nearly took my breath, and made my cheeks form a big smile.

"See the gold….this is an incredible gold find." In the past I had panned flower size gold that produced maybe an ounce of gold for every ton of dirt, but this discovery was a life changer. I stood up and thought about the whole situation. It appears this was a one-man operation. The man is dead. I wonder if he stashed his treasure nearby?

"I think I'll search this area really closely and see if I can come up with the victim's remains, or maybe bits of clothing or a wallet," I said, as I grabbed the rifle and crossed over to the far side of the small creek.

"Are you going to stay close to the cabin?" asked Gail.

I could see a worried look in Gail's eyes. "Come with me. I could use another set of eyes," I said. We walked in a series of widening circles; our efforts produced a half chewed leather belt and a beautiful Bowie knife in a scabbard.

I found some bear scat that had cloth mixed in with berry saturated feces. "This is bear poop," I said, as I bent over and picked up some fabric looking material from the pile of scat. I took the cloth material and washed it in the stream. It had the feel and appearance of a cotton shirt. It was becoming obvious a person bit the dust from a bear attack.

"It's my guess this man was killed and eaten by a bear; probably the same bear that attacked us. I bet the guy was engrossed in panning and a bear came up behind him." I was reminded of an incident on the Kenai Pennisula, in Alaska. The fish and game investigated a bear attack and came to the conclusion that a grizzly attacked a solo hiker while he was preparing his lunch. We continued to search the area but never found anything regarding a body. One lingering thought wouldn't go away.... Is there a stash of gold somewhere?

"If you were panning lots of gold where would you put it?" I asked Gail. Gail thought for a few seconds and then said, "I'd probably bury it." "Where?"

"Maybe in the cabin," said Gail.

I couldn't take my eyes off of the boot. I Thought, What a horrible way to die.

"Life seemed simple an hour ago, but that's all changed now. When we get home maybe we should contact a Hollywood producer and see if he would like to make a motion picture of this trip." Gail didn't smile but her facial expression seemed to agree.

"Do you know how valuable gold is today?"

"No," said Gail.

"Around $1700.00 an ounce. This guy might of buried his booty somewhere nearby." I thought, It wouldn't take long to search the cabin.

"We have time….I'm going to go back in the cabin and look around."

In about one minute I was back in the cabin and Gail was right beside me. I lit the lantern. I moved the bed and plunged the Bowie knife into the soil.

"If the gold is buried in here, the soil will be loose." The knife point hit hard packed dirt. Every square foot of the floor was hard until I poked where the stove was sitting.

"This dirt is soft," I said. The soft dirt was the first encouraging sign our hunt had produced.

"Cross your fingers." I said softly.

One more poke and I hit something solid about three inches in the dirt. I scraped the loose dirt off some wood planking. I thought, This is not a stick; its wood planking. This is a man thing; what's under the wood?

"There's a reason this wood is here," I said, as I lifted the four pieces of short flat boards.

"Check this out," I told Gail, as I removed the last board. There was a hole filled with small burlap material bags. Gail carried the lantern over closer to the hole. The light shone down on cotton sock size bags. The contents of the bags felt grainy as I squeezed each one. The bags were heavy...to heavy for dirt. I looked at Gail with a smile.... "I think our hunch was right...we'll know real soon."

I untied one of the bags and held the opening up to the lantern..... No doubt, I thought, as electricity seemed to suddenly start shooting through my veins.

Gail's lips formed the words, 'Oh my God!'

"What are you going to do?" Gail asked.

"I think I'll go pee and think about it," I said.

"I'm right behind you."

The forest suddenly seemed to have eyes and ears; as I moistened the soil I sensed that our discovered treasure was up for grabs to the first person who comes along....My first thought was, Whoever harvested the valuable mineral was obviously out of the picture. The small cabin appeared to only have one occupant, so it looked like a one person operation.

"Gold prospectors don't usually advertise where their dig is, so there's a good chance no one knows about this cabin, or the fact that the prospector even exists in this part of the wilderness. People are always going into the wilderness and no one ever hears from them again. If someone finds a nice fishing knife at a remote mountain lake, like I did a few years back, they wouldn't think twice about putting it in their pocket. An abandoned treasure belongs to the lucky soul who finds it. What do you think about my logic.... taking the gold and everything?"

Gail shrugged her shoulders. "Ok, I guess. Could we check with the authorities to find out if this guy filed a claim here?"

I thought about the question for a few seconds and said, "We can. Actually, we can scout up and down the creek and see if there are any mining claim stakes. I believe Canada requires that a filed claim is suppose to be identified with stakes. I mentioned to Gail, as we were walking, that Whitehorse was probably the place where those records were kept. We walked up the creek a quarter mile and didn't find any stakes.

"I'm going to take the gold and bury it ....maybe a couple hundred yards away from the cabin. We can't risk trying to carry all of that weight home. I don't want to explain how and where we got it.... I can come back later and carry it out. If we just leave it in the cabin the first person that discovers this place will put two and two together and figure this was a prospector's cabin."

"How much do you think it's worth?" asked Gail.

"One five pound bag is about 80 ounces, and if you multiply that times $1,700.00, it comes out to about one hundred and thirty six thousand dollars a bag; Fifteen bags times one hundred and thirty six thousand equals a little more than two million dollars."

"You're kidding?"

"No....for real," I said, with a smile.

I picked a spot to bury the gold...nearly a quarter mile from the cabin. I figured if someone comes along and occupies the cabin it would be better not to have any contact with them. Someday I can come back, unnoticed, and carry out the gold with no hassle of someone questioning my actions.

It took about an hour, using the Bowie knife, to dig a hole at the base of a fir tree. There was an unusual exposed rock next to the tree and I figured the rock and tree would be easy to relocate someday. There was only one more thing to do before we left to go back to the camp....I figured it would be a good idea to remove the wood pieces in the small stream......no sense in advertising and letting people know that someone was prospecting at the cabin site.

The hole in the cabin was filled in with rocks and dirt. The outside entrance boards were put back into position and covered with dirt.

"I've been thinking....I don't know about you, but I could put a couple of bags of gold to good use....I think we should take two bags each with us. We can conceal it well and not tell another living soul. What do you think?" I asked Gail.

Gail nodded in agreement. We were both physically burnt from a second day of high carb activity and starting to get hungry and we still had the mile hike back to the camp.

"I'm getting hungry and weaker by the minute." Gail took a lingering look at the cabin and the boot; she felt sadness for the poor soul who worked so hard and lost it all.

The mid-day warmer temperature pushed the mist and clouds higher and the threat of precipitation had lessened. Maybe tomorrow the weather will improve, I thought, as we headed back to the camp. We walked silently up the trail. The simple hike to get water had turned into a super roller coaster ride. Suddenly our lives had moved from the calm waters, of simply waiting to be rescued, into the fast moving, exhilarating, current of swirling choices and pathways. The shock of seeing a dismembered human being and then minutes later finding the gold begged for someone to say, 'Whoa, time-out! Let's sort this out.'

"This is all your fault!" said Gail, as she followed me up the winding trail.

I stopped and turned around. "What do you mean?"

"Well, before this trip, my life was simple and low key. Since I've known you, it's like, there's never been a dull moment. The crash; the bear attack, and now this morning....all that's happened in the last three hours; from rags to riches; from a slow life style at the Remington, to all this drama; seeing the beautiful country of Alaska and Canada from the airplane; sharing my life with you, and loving every minute of it; It's all your fault." I looked at Gail, and as her rambling sunk in, all I could do was give her a joy-filled smile.

Further up the trail, I stopped and said, "Hey, all this drama and excitement is way off the chart for me too. I hope life returns to a calmer pace; and, I might add, you are the reason the sun seems brighter and the birds seem so full of joy and laughter...in fact if I were the pie crust, you would be the filling. Gail smiled and rocked her shoulders as if she were listening to a good old rock and roll song.

"Is that so…you can be a charmer Mr. Parker", said Gail, with a glowing smile.

We would have really been perplexed if we knew half of the drama and fun that was ahead of us the next few years. I gave Gail a big hug and we continued on up the trail.

"Let's rest for a minute," I said.

"Do you think you'll go on a spending spree at Wallyworld?" I asked.

"No more Wallyworld….strickly Nordstroms from now on. How about you?" asked Gail.

"………I'm thinking….can't decide. Maybe I'll buy a plane and put the rest away in a can and bury it… maybe I'll spread it out among the kids."

"I hope I get home safe and sound and get the chance to spend it," said Gail.

"You will."

"Our kids and grand kids are going to talk about this for a long time…. I wish I could call and tell them not to worry," said Gail.

"Ready?" I said, as I extended a hand to help Gail stand-up.

The closer we got to the top of the ridge, I saw more breaks in the overcast. The patches of blue sky was a good sign that tomorrow might be our day for an exciting exit.

For me, enjoying the moment, following the crash, was nearly non-existent until this point. Looking at mother nature's beautiful flowers and trees, swaying in the breeze, made me feel one with the beautiful environment. Thank you Lord, for the pleasing sense of happiness I'm feeling right now, I thought.

My prayer made me think of a song sung by the late Karen Carpenter.

'Top of The World', was on the top hit chart for some time. I was feeling on top of another mountain, in more ways than one.

'Such a feelings comin over me; there is wonder in most everything I see. I'm on top of the world looking down on creation and the only explanation I can find, is the love that I've found ever since she's been around…..Her love puts me at the top of the world.' Funny how history has repeated itself….I was incredibly in love with another woman, as a young man, in fact the soil still contains the seed…the difference now is the nourishment is being poured on new seed …..funny how that song fell off the shelf….the words really fit, I thought.

3ᴿᴰ DAY NOON WHITEHORSE

"This is Hal. How are you doing?"

"Keeping busy, what's up?" asked Fred, as he paused from working on his dental patient.

"It looks like a go for tomorrow morning."

"We're ready to go," said Fred.

"Looks like good weather. The radar shows a clear pattern for tomorrow morning. Alert everyone for a 6:30 stand-by. Tell everyone to be tanked up and ready for a meeting at the Watson Lake tower at 7:30. I want to be in the air no later than 8:00." replied Jake.

"How many people are we talking about?" asked Fred "Two; a retired man and woman from Anchorage, Alaska."

"Ok. I'll tell everyone to be expecting a call around 5:30 A.M. You want us to be on the ground at Watson Lake no later than 7:30, correct?"

"That's correct," said Hal.

PHONE CALL TO WILLIAM, PRINCE GEORGE

"Hello Mr. Parker, Mr. Wilcox, from Whitehorse. I just called to bring you up to date…. the weather kept us on the ground today, but we plan to be up and looking for your father and his friend starting at 8:00 in the morning." "What time do you think you will be in the area where the second airstrip is?" asked William.

"By 9:00, I would estimate."

"So we might possibly be getting a call around mid-day tomorrow?"

"Yes, that's a possibility. One way or another you will hear from me tomorrow," replied Hal Wilcox. William took a deep breath and replied, "Thank you for the call." "Hang in there," replied Hal.

William hung up the phone and thought…. God if you are for real, please be with Gail and Dad.

DAY 3 MID-DAY, LEFT CABIN, RETURNING TO CAMP

The trail was less steep the closer we got to the top of the ridge. The shiny green trees were swaying from the front that seemed to be pushing the gray saturated clouds towards the north. The endorphins were really kicking in. My mood was certainly improved from the time we started down into the canyon. The rifle, gold, and the sun popping through the clouds and Gail near my side added up to a very pleasant hike back to camp.

"Almost there," I said.

"Do you mind if I take a nap after lunch?" asked Gail.

"I'll join you.

"Look at that!" I said, as I stopped and pointed out to Gail two small spotted fawns and their proud protective mother standing in the trail curiously watching our progress as we hiked up the game trail.

"Oh, how beautiful, said Gail.

"I think we've seen the last of the rain for a while. If the weather continues to improve there's a good chance we'll see some planes tomorrow."

After all that had transpired the past two days, a messed up campsite would not have been a surprise, I thought, as we approached the white ashes of the camp fire. The camp looked the same; the food pack was still suspended up in the tree. The platform was undisturbed. The tarp protected our bedding. I stoked up the fire and a hot hardy meal set the stage for a nice afternoon nap.

"Let me climb up by myself," said Gail, as she climbed up the twenty feet to the platform.

"Good job," I said, right behind her. The sleeping bags felt warm and secure. I hung the rifle on a limb within easy arms reach. My nap did not come easy; so much had occurred the past couple of hours that would change the course of our lives....would it be for the better? I thought.

"When we get up it'll be time for a bingo game at the Remington; I wish we were there now," said Gail.

Gail was one to get involved in all the social activities. She memorized what days various activities were played. I could participate or go for a bike ride; exercise helped balance my metabolism and calmed me down. Gail preferred the social interaction of games. I enjoyed being with Gail, plain and simple.

Two hours later I flipped off the bag and looked up to hear a raven having a conversation with another raven. The raven's black feathers cast a shiny glow in spite of the dimly lit mid-day sky. The big birds strutted around with a confident flair as they watched us on the platform. As I watched the pretty, proud looking birds stare at me, I thought, I may be more intelligent than you, but along with that goes a big load of responsibilities. The Tlingit Indians, who fought the Russians fiercely, in Southeast Alaska, revered the raven. They appreciated the intelligence, color and strong features of the bird.

I laced my boots, grabbed the rifle and climbed off the platform. I wonder if that bear is close by, I thought, as I picked up the blood trail and walked in the direction the bear had walked; about a hundred yards from the camp I spotted something brown and furry; barely visible, behind a three foot thick log. There was no movement and I was guessing it was the culprit that attacked us the night before. I better get back to camp before some girl misses me, I thought, as I turned around and headed towards camp. Gail had just crawled out of her bag and was looking down when I walked into the camp. "Have a good nap?"

Gail answered with a resounding, "No, I had a GREAT nap."

"All right! Come on down. I have something interesting to show you." Oh boy...what did he find now, thought Gail. No lack of testosterone in my system, I thought, as I watched Gail nimbly step limb to limb down the tree.

"Would you agree, it's been an interesting day so far?" I asked.

Gail twisted her back and grimaced with pain as she commented, "Every day hanging around you is an interesting day. My back is sore."

"I know what will help," I said, as I lowered the pack and got some pain pills.

"Here, take two of these....they really help soothe my aches and pains."

"You mean if I take two pills it will help your aches and pains, or do you mean they will help my pain?" "What?" I replied.

"Never mind," said Gail, as she chuckled.

"What's this interesting thing you wanted to show me?" asked Gail.

"It's big, brown and furry."

"Is it dead?" Gail asked. I nodded my head.

"I followed the blood trail. I'd like to retrieve my arrows...Maybe I can take home a bear claw as a souvenir to share with the kids."

"What if it's not dead?" asked Gail.

"It wouldn't be anywhere near us if it was alive."

"I'll go along... but I'm not going near that animal," said Gail.

I picked up the rifle and started walking in the direction of the bear.

"See the brown fur, just past the big log? Stay here. I'll walk over and check it out." It couldn't of survived those four arrows, I thought.

I walked to the end of the log; it was the bear; an arrow was sticking out about six inches from the animal's lower back. Seeing the arrow made a cold chill run up my spine....those memories came flooding back. The bear had collapsed belly down on all four of it's feet. I threw a softball size rock that rolled up and hit the carcass; there was no movement. The animal was dead. I felt a measure of sadness for this beautiful creature that was simply pursuing another meal.

"Come on over. It's dead." Gail Slowly walked to the end of the log where she kept a safe, thirty foot distance from the animal. She was content to hang back at a distance as I cut out a few claws, using the Bowie knife. I found a long pole and pried the bear over on its side. I stuck the pole between the bear and the log and was able to get the leverage to move the heavy beast onto its side. I was able to extract one arrow by pulling it out of the back; another pull of the stick and the bear rolled clear over on its back. The canine teeth were two inches long.

As we walked back to camp I thought about the three arrows that were still in the animals body; maybe I'll find them later, when I come back to get the gold. I'm going to hang this arrow on the wall at home and put it beside a picture of a grizzly.

The clouds were clearly breaking up; there were small pockets of blue sky. There was a gentle breeze and it seemed the storm was passing through the area rather than hanging around like the night before.

"If the weather clears up, and they find us tomorrow, what do you think will occur?" asked Gail, as we sat on our bench next to the fire.

"I've never been in a search and rescue….My guess is, after they spot us, they will try to communicate…maybe drop a note, or something. I'll put my shirt on a stick and wave it when they fly over; this will get their attention and let them know we need help. They probably will land at the closest gravel strip and hike over to us."

"I'm excited…The sooner the better," said Gail, as she squeezed my hand.

"Tomorrow we're going to need dry wood, so I guess I better get busy cutting and gathering." Two hours later the pine needles were stacked up about four feet high.

"That's enough, I hope," I said.

As I sipped some water and looked at the rifle, it dawned on me that maybe Gail didn't know how to shoot a rifle.

"Do you know how to shoot a rifle?"

"No. I shot a hand-gun once."

"You're going to get your first lesson," I said.

"Why?" asked Gail. I looked at Gail, over the top of my glasses… "Because something could happen to me and I want you to be able to protect yourself; does that make sense?"

I explained how to hold, aim and shoot the rifle; the use of working the bolt to eject the spent cartridge, and then chambering the next round.

"Ok, aim at that pinecone over by the tree and hold the stock close to your shoulder." I moved to stand behind her as she lifted the heavy gun and aimed. The sound echoed through the trees sending birds screeching into the air. "Ouch! That hurt," said Gail, as she handed the rifle to me. "That was loud."

"Yeah. It takes a few shots to get use to it. Ok, now take the bolt and lift and pull it back….good; now push it forward and pull down on the bolt; good; careful now. If you pull the trigger the gun will shoot. Think you can do it?" I asked.

"Yeah, I think so.….I know so," said Gail, as she rubbed her shoulder, thinking, no way I'm shooting that thing again, unless absolutely necessary.

I put the rifle aside and we both sat on the log next to the popping fire. The clouds were opening and more blue sky and sunlight was illuminating the forest.

"The clouds are nearly high enough now to fly." I looked at Gail, took her hand and said, "I'm ready to be rescued; how about you?"

"Amen!" said Gail, as her smile and shiny blue eyes met my stare. We both, simultaneously, reached out for each other, acknowledging a mutual need to give and receive love and comfort. Our lips shyly met. Holding her in my arms seemed to drain all the pain out of my aching body. Energy suddenly flooded my soul. Our friendship was undeniably growing, like a snowball rolling down the mountain.

Gail felt a comfort and contentment, that could not be put into words.…I wish this could last forever, she thought.

As I lowered the food pack I had a thought. "If we start running low on food we can go raid the cabin." "That's true," said Gail.

"It was nearly 5:30 in the afternoon. I wasn't very hungry, for some strange reason, but I thought it would be a good time to heat some water and eat one or two of the dehydrated dinner packages.

"Are you hungry?" I asked.

"A little. How about a delicious Rib Eye Steak; with a salad and baked potato, plus sour cream and real butter," suggested Gail.

"Sounds good to me," I said.

The hot spicy meal was tasty and filling, but the wilderness dinner was a far cry from eating with family and the security of familiar surroundings.

"I would enjoy this food a whole lot more if I had a thirty four foot RV, with a pop-out and a satellite dish and fresh coffee……how about you?" I said. Gail nodded her head and gave me an encouraging smile that reflected a spirit of guarded optimism.

The rest of the evening consisted in small talk around the fire and watching the cloud layer break-up. I looked at my watch and said, "It's 9:00 o'clock. You ready to hit the sack?" "Yes." I hope we have a peaceful night, thought Gail.

3ᴿᴰ DAY, EVENING, WILLIAM'S HOME

"I'm going to have a glass of wine. Care for some?" asked William.

"No thanks," replied Stephannie.

"I'm staying home tomorrow. I'll call the boss in the morning. I hope they find Dad and Gail parked on a runway tomorrow morning. We might be getting a call before noon."

"I hope you're right," said Stephannie

3ᴿᴰ DAY EVENING, SACK TIME

"You need any help?" I asked, as Gail walked over to climb the tree.

"Nope. I can do it, but thank you."

We walked over to the tree together and I patted Gail on the back and said, "What a girl...Do you still remember how to shoot the rifle?"

"You bet." There's no way I'm going to shoot that thing again, thought Gail.

"You just want me to suffer some more pain, don't you?" joked Gail.

I squeezed Gail's shoulder and swatted her on the butt, and said, "No comment."

I pulled the food pack up in the tree and headed for the platform. There was another hour of daylight after Gail and I climbed onto the platform. The view from the platform felt much safer.

"I can't remember the last time I found a few million in gold, can you?" I asked.

"It's been the biggest payday of my life?" replied Gail.

"I'm really glad you built this platform. Gold is no good if you're dead, like that poor guy," said Gail.

"I can hear your grand-kids now; "Ga Ga, would you tell us again about your camping trip?" I said.

The word "grand kids" had a sweet ring. Somehow the word brought being home again closer to reality for Gail.

It will be nice to have Bailey on my lap and giving her a hug and seeing her smile and winking eyes, thought Gail.

"If the sky clears up we might be looking at getting out of this mess tomorrow. How's that sound?" "That would be wonderful," said Gail.

"It just might happen. We have plenty of food and we are secure up here….We've just got to be patient. Waiting is the hard part," I said.

After a few big yawns we both decided to crawl into our warm, snug, sleeping bag. Late in the night nature called and I flipped on my headlamp. My watch showed 12:15. The night is going fast, I thought. The night sky revealed lots of shiny stars. The crickets were humming away and a commercial plane could be heard off in the distance, probably up thirty five thousand feet in the air. At 5:30 it was light enough to read a book. I looked at Gail and thought, she's lucky she has a healthy bladder; climbing all the way to the ground to go pee would be a pain. The fire was down to nothing but coals. There wasn't a trace of smoke. No reason to get up now, I thought. The clouds were much higher and small patches of gray clouds were drifting from south to north. It looks good, I thought, as I crawled back into the bag with a smile of excitement. Not a whole lot to do; build up the fire; cook breakfast; put up the smoke signal around 8:00 o'clock…. Yipeee, I thought, as I drifted back to a blissful sleep.

4TH DAY THE RESCUE

7:20…..Time to get up, I thought, as I flipped back the covers and viewed the new day through blurry, sleepy eyes.

I slipped on my shoes, crawled over and shook Gail.

"Time to rise and shine," I said, as I watched Gail flap the sleeping bag and expose her head. "Sleep good?" I asked.

"Yes…speaking of shine…it's going to be a beautiful day," said Gail, as she looked up at the blue, cloudless sky. The morning air was cold. The fire was going to feel good. I was anxious to get everything going; the fire, breakfast, my cold stiff body, time itself.

I threw wood on the fire and said, "Zippity do da, Zippity-A, Planes will soon be coming our way." "Think so?" asked Gail.

"Well, if we were playing cards I'd bet five pennies on it." "And why is that?" asked Gail.

I looked up at the sky….."See the blue sky?" Gail nodded her head. "Nature is saying we haven't been forgotten.

Help will soon be on the way."

"Ok…I'll believe it when I see the rocking wings."

This is the day. This is the day that the Lord hath made…..I will rejoice, I will rejoice and be glad in it. I was singing this song in my head as I watched Gail getting food out of the pack.

"I don't know why, but I can't get that bear out of my mind. The more I think about it, the more I get the feeling it was our misfortune to crash on his turf at a time when "people eating" was preferable over berries and bugs and plants. I really think he killed the prospector."

My watch showed 8:00 o'clock. "Time to stoke up the fire and start putting up the smoke."

The last comment stirred excitement in Gail's heart. I hope you're right, thought Gail. The hope of regaining control of one's life again was like seeing the sun's early rise; it's coming soon because darkness is losing its grip. Hope was coming in small steps. Gail wanted so much to see the rescuers arrive, but she knew she needed to accept the moment in small increments; disappointment is less painful this way. When her senses of sight and vision and sound became reality, then and only then could she release the rapturous feelings of joy.

WHITEHORSE, CIVIL AIR PATROL

The Whitehorse Civil Air Patrol was headed by Hal Wilcox. This was a group of private pilot volunteers who enjoy flying their planes and donating their time helping others in need. Hal's good friend, Fred Summers, was prepared to cancel his dental appointments if Jake called and said, "Let's do it."

The phone rang early. "This is Hal. The weather's good. Round up the gang and let's all meet at 7:30 at the Watson Lake Terminal."

"Roger, roger," said Fred.

Fred's reputation for being a hot shot snow mobile racer was known far and wide. He trained year-round and raced in the thousand mile snow mobile Tesoro Iron Horse Race every winter. There were four pilots from Watson Lake; two teachers; one business owner, and one retired police officer. The entire crew of six, enjoyed the outdoor recreational activities of the beautiful Canadian Rocky wilderness. The men prided themselves in wilderness survival. They were disciplined and competent in their own right. Flying was a joy they all shared; rescuing others was a way to put their skills to use.

The men had a common thread in their lives....they were all united in their belief about who created the wilderness, which they dearly loved. God was their co-pilot in all aspects of life.

WATSON LAKE

"Listen up; thanks guys for your help. We are looking for a senior couple from Anchorage, Alaska; we have reason to believe they went down in the upper Williston Lake area, near the second gravel airstrip; about an hour from here. When we reach the north end of the lake, the six of us will spread out about two hundred yards apart. Fred, I want you to fly along the lake shore and I will be the farthest west; everyone fill in between Fred and I; use 126.7 and feel free to speak if you have a question or have something important to say; monitor 121.5....you might pick up an ELT signal. If the plane is located the spotter needs to stay over the wreckage until I can get there. When I spot the plane everyone else go to the nearest strip and land; I will get there as soon as possible; any questions?" Everyone eyed Hal and shook their heads.

"Ok, let's have a prayer and get after it." There were no words spoken as the men walked through the building on the way to the parked planes. The sectional map showed the lake was 180 degrees out of the Watson Lake airport.

"Fred, taxiing for take-off on runway 090 Watson Lake strip." The rest of the pilots visually lined up behind Fred and followed him onto the runway. The time of takeoff was 8:00 o'clock in the morning.

I tossed the pine needles on the fire and in about ten minutes the smoke was high enough to be seen by pilots nearly a hundred miles away.

Fifteen minutes into the flight the pilots were able to see the lake and smoke on the far horizon. The terrain below was a broad dense carpet of green forest. Fred was in the lead and everyone fanned out to his right.

Hal Wilcox was about a half mile west of Fred. The planes were about a 1,000 feet above the tree tops.

"That smoke could be our man...cross your fingers, Hal out." The southern horizon revealed smoke coming out of the forest. The morning sky was bright blue, and the wind was calm. The forest was virgin, no roads, no trace of man's footprint, and totally green in every direction.

Gail grabbed my arm and said, "Listen!" Gail's hearing was better than mine and she first heard the sound of a plane. We both froze and turned our heads. I smiled and thought, right on schedule. The sound seemed to be coming from the north. I grabbed the pole and attached my shirt. We both were holding our breath as the sound steadily got louder.

Hal's path was taking him straight towards the smoke. The lake was directly below Fred and he could see the first gravel strip. The radio was silent as the planes had descended to five hundred feet above the trees. Everyone could see the smoke.

Let this be our people, thought Hal, as he got closer to the source of the ascending plume of smoke. Any second now, thought Hal.

"Bingo!" Hal shouted, when he spotted a figure waving a flag on the edge of a meadow; two people, to be exact.

They were excitedly waving their arms as Hal buzzed over them.

"This is Hal...Two people spotted on the ground."

"I see the wreckage," reported another pilot.

"This is Hal. Everyone land back at the second airstrip. I will be there shortly."

Gail's eyes watered as the plane nosed down, rocked it's wings, and flew a hundred feet over their heads. Oh God, thank you, thought Gail, as tears welled up in her eyes.

We looked at each other and then engaged in a huge celebratory hug.

"Now I think I know how ET felt when his people came to pick him up," I said, with tears forming in my eyes. "Hal grabbed the walkie talkie and stuffed it in a cardboard box. He taped the box tightly shut. On the second pass he popped open his side window and tossed out the box; it landed in the middle of the meadow. I ran over and opened the box, expecting to find a note.

"Huh?" I said, when I discovered the walkie talkie radio. I keyed the mike and said,

"Hello."

"Mr. Parker?"

"Yes," I said.

"You guys ok?"

"We're fine…no injuries." Gail walked over by my side. She heard the conversation and tears of joy flowed from her eyes, as she realized their rescue was really happening.

"Are you both healthy enough to walk a few miles?" asked Hal.

"Yes."

"Ok, here's what I need you to do. The lake is east of you about a mile; follow the ridge line down to the lake and hang a left and go a mile or two until you reach the gravel strip. We'll meet you there. Use the radio if you have any problem." instructed Jake, as he made a tight spiral above the two.

"Roger. Go to the lake and turn left," I repeated.

"Roger. See you in a few hours," said Hal. Whew…no injuries; I wish they all ended this short and sweet, thought Hal, as he turned to take a look at the wreckage. The wreckage was in a tight cluster of trees; it would have been hard to spot that plane, thought Hal. He took off the wings…textbook landing.

I explained to Gail that we had been asked to hike to the airstrip a few miles away. I thought about what we should take…..I'll roll up the sleeping bags and include the archery equipment and wrap them tightly in the tent canvas and leave them on the platform. I can come back this summer and carry them out.

It took about ten minutes to tightly wrap the bags in the waterproof canvas. l crawled down the tree and walked over to the fire and pulled the charred branches over to the wet meadow grass. I piled up dirt on the charcoal embers.

"That'll do it."

I looked up at the tree platform one more time, and said, "Say good-by to our penthouse." Gail smiled and said, "Come on let's go."

I slung on the thirty pound back pack, (including the four bags of gold), grabbed the rifle, grabbed Gail's hand and sang the words, 'I'm going home, I'm going home.' I remembered singing this Tony Orlando and Dawn song when I left Vietnam.

The adrenaline made the first part of the hike feel like we were walking on air. The hike towards the lake took us directly by the plane; seeing the plane for the last time stirred up melancholy feelings for me. Gail thought about her two suit cases of scattered clothes in the back seat of the plane...Oh well, they can be replaced, she thought.

"Oh," said Gail. "Can you reach the Alaska shirts we got for Stephannie and William?" "No problem. I forgot all about those shirts," I said.

Seeing the inside of the cockpit, and looking at the avionics and the dual yokes made me feel sad...a lot of good memories. I spotted the ELT as I shuffled through the clothes. The ELT toggle switch was in the neutral position. I didn't push it far enough, I thought. I grabbed the two shirts and the cell phone and backed out of the interior of the plane.

"Oh! We've got to take those," I said, as I spotted the pink kitty cat pajamas.

Gail asked me what I was talking about. "Your pink pajamas...we can't leave those behind." I said.

Gail blushed and said, "Thank you...We ought to get these two shirts monogrammed, 'WE SURVIVED'." "Good idea," I said.

"Hey, we are going to need our passports and the planes registration papers." said Gail.

"Boy, you're right! Guess there's no doubt who has the brains in this group," I said.

The hike soon began a gradual descent as we followed the ridge towards the lake. The game trails criss-crossed in every direction and the walking was an easy down hill walk.

"See the lake," I said, as I pointed towards the blue lake that was visible through the cluster of fir trees. At the juncture where we needed to turn left we were standing on the bank of a fast moving stream; the water was dangerously fast and deep. We stood together looking at the white water and I said, "This is the same stream that went by the cabin. We'll need to follow the creek and hopefully find a safe place to cross."

"Ready?"

"Lead on," Gail said.

The heavy snow melt every spring had exposed huge boulders in the creek.

"Look at that," I said, as I pointed at a three foot thick pine tree stretched across the entire width of the creek. "That's our bridge."

"You expect me to walk across that?" asked Gail.

"No. We'll scoot across on our butts; one inch at a time; just pretend you're on the school playground. My daughter and I crossed over a swollen stream this way when we were hiking in the mountains of California."

I figured if I led, it would give Gail the courage to scoot along behind me. We were half way across with our legs hanging down towards the fast moving, white foamy water, when I stopped and said, "Catch your breath. You're doing great." The noise from the water was loud, and Gail preferred not to look down for fear the powerful moving stream might make her dizzy. Thank you God this "camping trip" is almost over. They are going to be floored when we tell our story, thought Gail. Gail reflected how she would soon be sharing the details of their past few days with her family.

"Could you dig out two more pain pills when you get a chance? My knee... my whole body is aching," asked Gail.

"Ok. Ready to get across this log?" I asked.

"Ok."

"Whew!" I shouted, after we both slid off the log onto the ground. I looked at Gail and said, "For two old retired people, we're doing pretty good." We hugged and patted each other on the back.

"You have pine pitch on your butt." said Gail.

"Really?" I said, as I rubbed my sticky backside.

"Let me see you....Turn around....You have a little too; rub some sand on it, otherwise we'll mess up someone's plane seats."

"Can you believe it?" I said, as I got Gail her pain pills. "Whitehorse today, and we'll be able to call the kids and put their minds to rest."

"Yes!" said Gail

AT THE GRAVEL AIRSTRIP

The pilots landed at the end of the runway farthest from the lake. The men got out of their planes and sat down at the base of a pine tree, waiting for Hal to land; they didn't have long to wait. Hal lifted his clinched fist, as he walked towards the men with a smile. "Our hunt is over. They are both alive and well."

The man, who spotted the plane, spoke up. "He put the plane between two trees and took off the wings." "Yeah… he did a good job," said Hal. "I talked to them with the walkie-talkies and they said they were fine and that they could walk out. They should be here in a couple of hours. I wish all of our rescues could be this easy." The men pulled out their lunches and tarps and proceeded to make themselves comfortable.

The walking was easy going as we followed the game trails, which took us towards our destination. There were open areas of sand that exposed a large number of different animal tracks; it was easy to distinguish between bear, cougar and deer tracks. The sun felt lusciously warm and soothing in the open areas. The prospect of being rescued made the long hike seem like a pleasant, short walk in the park. The lake over our right shoulder was very scenic. I frequently looked ahead to try and spot the airstrip where the planes would be parked.

"Let's take a break," I said, as I took off my back pack. "Your knee sore?" I asked.

"Yes. The pills haven't kicked in yet."

"Mr. Parker can you hear me?"

"Hello. Yes, I hear you loud and clear," I replied.

"Do you need any assistance?"

"We're doing fine…..I figure we'll spot the airstrip in a few more minutes."

"Ok. I estimate it's about a two and a half mile hike."

"Gotcha. I will call you if we have any problem."

"Roger. See you in a little while," said Hal.

The rest of the hike had several dips and inclines and I was hoping, for both of us, that we would soon spot the airstrip.

"There they are!" I said, as I pointed through the trees to the tail end of one of the planes. "Ten more minutes and we'll be there."

Thank God, thought Gail, as she took in a deep breath.

The walk down the bank and onto the airstrip was a little tricky, but once we got to the packed gravel strip it was easy walking. "Isn't that a beautiful sight," I said, as we walked towards the men. Seeing the parked planes and the men who came walking over to greet us, brought on a flood of tears to Gail's eyes. Seeing those planes and the rescue crew reminded Gail of how she felt when she came out of the tight claustrophobic MRI tunnel…the stress seemed to fall from her mind immediately.

The rescue party was curious as to what kind of people they had found; were they greenhorns or sourdough spunky folks? A few questions soon answered their curiosity.

"Good to see you folks! This is Gail and I'm Bill." Everyone exchanged hand-shakes.

"Mind if we sit down?" I asked, as I took Gail's hand and sat down on a tarp, near a cluster of small fir trees.

I figured they were wondering what happened, so I started the conversation by saying, "We might of had a fuel problem. The engine died and I couldn't get it going again. I was able to put the plane between two trees and we were fortunate to walk away with just a big knot on my head."

"Tell them what happened to your shirt," said Gail. My lips curled up a bit and I closed my eyes; because of fatigue and being asked to recall that ugly attack, my facial expression was probably perceived as a painful request.

"Our first day we noticed a lot of grizzly bear sign. The plane seats and water bottles were destroyed by a bear not long after we crashed. I built a tree platform the afternoon of our first day and around 9:30 in the evening we were visited by a full grown grizzly. It refused to leave when I yelled at it. It approached within ten feet of us and proceeded to come right up the tree and attack us. I threw my shirt down to the ground hoping to draw the bear out into the open. I was forced to kill it. We would have probably been killed if we had been on the ground. The bear had no fear."

"Bear are unpredictable, that's for sure," said Hal. "Lucky for you, you had that phone conversation with your daughter just before you had the engine failure. She gave the information to your son and he called me about an hour later."

I smiled and shook my head. I thought, Good for that boy.

"Yeah, I figured him right." I took a deep breath, and said, "It wasn't our time to go… that was a scary crash," I said, as I looked at Gail.

Got that right, thought Hal, as he nodded his head.

"Well, you made it through this storm…I guess He has more work for you to do. Ready to get back to the land of hot showers and soft beds?" asked Hal.

I looked at Gail and answered, "Is the Pope Catholic?"

Everyone huddled around shaking our hands and hugging Gail. The love was so strong, as all our souls meshed under a warm cloud of gratitude.

Hal looked around at all of the men…"Well, I'm going home with a good feeling. Thank you all for taking on this mission. Let's end it with a short prayer."

"Thank you God that these two will be able to continue to witness to others about your mercy and grace. Help us all to reflect your love, in our homes and abroad, as this couple has done here today. In Jesus's name…..Let's continue to monitor 126.7 for the next hour or so. Take care….Fred, I'll call you tomorrow," said Hal.

The men picked up their gear and walked over to their planes. "Would you care for a soda, or something to eat?" asked Hal. I looked at Gail and said, "That would be great. Thank you."

"Let's put your gear in the plane and get you folks back to Whitehorse."

"Nice plane," I said, admiring Hal's tail-dragger airplane. Hal's plane was a blue and white Cessna 185, with tundra tires. It was a five passenger plane that's very well designed for short field take-offs and landings.

"Thanks. It provides me at least one good hunting and fishing trip every year. Gail would you mind sitting in the back seat?" asked Hal.

"No problem."

Hal put his seat belt on and looked around to make sure his two passengers were belted in.

"Here we go."

The plane climbed to about 5,000 feet above the terrain and leveled off.

"Would you folks like to use my cell phone and call your kids?"

I looked at Gail and said, "Go for it."

Gail's hands were shaking with emotion and fatigue as she dialed the cell phone number.

"Hello," said Gail's daughter, Joni.

"This is your Mom."

"Oh my God! Brian, it's Mom! How are you?" asked Joni, as tears blurred her eyes.

"I'm fine," said Gail, as tears rolled down her cheeks. "Bill and I crashed in the forest and neither one of us got seriously hurt. The search and rescue people just picked us up and we are flying to Whitehorse. We are sore and tired and dirty....I'll call you later this evening from the lodge. I have a story to tell that will be hard to believe. We are both fine, just a few frazzled nerves. Is everyone there ok?"

"We've been worried sick. I mean really sick. Bill's son said today we would be hearing something. You're really OK?"

"Yes," Gail said, as she gazed at a bright shiny panorama of lakes, forest and mountains. "Bill was knocked out for a while, but he came out of it a few minutes later."

"I hope you never get in a plane again," cried Joni, as she hugged her husband Bryan.

"Ok honey, we're safe now and things will only get better. I'll call you later this evening. I love you all."

"Love you Mom." said Joni. Gail handed the phone to me, as she rubbed her eyes with tissue paper. I'm not fearful of flying, thought Gail, as she thought about Joni's last comment.

"Hello," answered William.

"I'm alive and well," I said.

"Tell me what happened?" William signaled to Stephannie and lipped 'Dad,' as he pushed the speaker button. "The engine died and I couldn't restart it. I crash landed the plane in the forest. Neither one of us got hurt seriously. I was knocked unconscious for a couple of minutes. The search and rescue spotted us about 9:00 o'clock this morning. We were asked to walk about three miles to an airstrip, where the planes landed and waited for us to show up. We are flying to Whitehorse now."

"Everyone will be thankful this had a happy ending....Did you meet Hal Wilcox?" asked William.

"Sure did, in fact we are in his plane and he's sitting next to me."

"Would you please tell him I said 'Thank you'. I've been talking with him the past three days," said William. "I sure will. Is everyone ok there?"

"Yeah. We've been worried sick about you and Gail."

"We survived a horrific crash and a bear attack, but we are fine now......I'll call you this evening, if you're going to be home."

"I think I might take Stef out to dinner and try to calm our nerves." "Good idea. I'll call you tomorrow evening," I said. "I want to hear all the details; Stef wants to say hi."

"Sure, put her on."

"Hi Dad."

"Hello. I'm sorry I hung up so abruptly last time we talked. You did a good job letting the authorities know where we were....thank God for our short conversation."

"You can't imagine what a relief it is to know you and Gail are safe and not hurt," said Stephannie.

"You can't imagine how good it feels to be in this plane....A hot shower, a soft bed and a good dinner is all I can think about."

"It sounds like you've had quite an adventure," said Stephannie.

"Boy, you got that right. We've run a gamut of emotions; a spoiled trip; loss of a plane and surviving a ferocious bear attack. We're tired, and sore from the hike to get to the airplane pick-up site; we need a good nights rest and some Aleve and we'll be fine. I'll call tomorrow evening and tell you the whole story. Would you mind calling the girls?"

"I will, as soon as, like now," said Stephannie.

"I better let you go. Love you guys."

"Love you, too, Dad, bye."

"Dad and Gail are alive and well." replied Stephannie. Myndi, Bill's oldest daughter, filled her lungs and slowly let out a sigh; she was sitting at her desk, in her high school classroom, as the tears rolled down her cheeks. All of our kids were expecting a call any minute, so the phone ring grabbed Myndi's attention with a spiked sense of anticipation. She turned the chair with her back to the students.

"The engine died and they crash- landed in the forest. Dad was knocked unconscious and Gail woke him up a few minutes later. He said something about being attacked by a bear. They are flying to Whitehorse right now and Dad is going to call later. Their cell phone batteries are low now. Maybe now we all can get some sleep," said Stephannie.

"Thanks for the call. I'll call Lilly and Sonnet; four more days of school. It sounds like Dad whacked a few trees." "He said he had one hell of a story to tell," said Stephannie. "Maybe he'll give up flying?" said Myndi.

"You think so?"

"No…. Love you sister. I have about 35 curious sets of ears that are going to want to hear this story," said Myndi.

Lilly was driving down a country road and looking for an address of two prospective foster parents. Lilly saw Myndi's name on the cell phone. Dad was the first thing that popped in her mind. Oh, she thought, I hope this is not bad.

"Hello."

"Hey, great news! Dad and Gail were found a few hours ago and they are alive and well."

"All right! What happened?" asked Lilly, as she pulled off onto the shoulder of the road and stopped in a cloud of dust.

"The engine died and Dad put the plane into the forest. He was knocked unconscious and Gail revived him a few minutes later. They survived the crash with no broken bones and later were attacked by a bear."

"Leave it up to Dad....never a dull moment," laughed Lilly. "How did they get rescued?"

"I don't know. They are flying to Whitehorse now and you might be able to get them on Dad's cell phone tonight."

Lilly took a deep breath and said, "Mom will want to hear the good news....I'll call her in a little while. I'll call Sonnet also," said Lilly.

"Ok. I'm in the middle of a class, so I'll talk to you later," said Myndi.

"Later," said Lilly.

Sonnet was in the office baby-sitting a German Shepherd pup, that belonged to her boss. She shouted when Lilly told her we were safe and sound. Thank you Lord, she thought, when she heard the good news.

"You might be able to get him on his cell phone this evening; right now they are flying to Whitehorse." "Did you hear what happened?" asked Sonnet.

"The engine died and they crash landed in the forest. Something hit Dad and knocked him out and Gail woke him up a few minutes later. Get this...they were attacked by a bear."

"You're kidding," said Sonnet.

"No. They really were attacked by a bear."

"Poor Gail," said Sonnet.

"I've got to go. Talk to you later," said Lilly.

4ᵀᴴ DAY, WHITEHORSE BOUND

"My son told me to thank you," I said to Hal.

Hal shrugged his shoulders, and said, "This is the most rewarding part about my job. Helping folks, like you two; makes my job a whole lot more interesting."

"That was a smart thing, building a tree platform," said Hal.

"I don't know if it's global warming, or the fact that more people are encroaching in bear habitat, but I've read where bear attacks are occurring more often. Last summer in Alaska, above the Arctic Circle, a couple were attacked while asleep in the middle of the night. They were well armed, but the bear hit so hard and aggressively, they didn't have time to defend themselves."

Hal nodded his head. "Usually bear will run if you give them a chance."

"That's been my experience with them, up until now. This bear seemed to have us on his dinner menu from the get go."

"What kind of work do you do?" asked Hal.

"School teacher, retired," I said. "Will I need to file a report with the tower authorities and police?" "The aviation folks will need a report; I don't know about the police," said Hal.

"My insurance company will probably need an accident report, so I better hit both places. We are going to check into the lodge by the airstrip."

"I can run you over there," said Hal.

The flight was smooth and the landscape never looked better. Gail closed her eyes and took a nap. My foot was hurting from the hike and

I also had heavy eyes. My watch showed 4:35 when Hal radioed the Whitehorse tower to let them know he was in-bound from the east.

"Could you tell the tower I will come in tomorrow to fill out a report?" Hal nodded his head. I squeezed Gail's hand. It was an awesome feeling to see the airport and know we were going to be back on safe terra firma in a few minutes.

At the lodge Hal carried the back pack into the lobby. Hal stuck out his hand and said, "I wish you a happy life. You did a good job of taking care of your lady."

"You guys risked your lives, and words cannot express how grateful we are," I said.

"God did His part, you did your part and we were blessed to have the opportunity to bring things to a happy ending; all in a days work… call it Christian Canadian hospitality…being a good neighbor, ya might say," said Hal, as he shook my hand.

As Hal walked away I thought, That was a profound statement; short and to the point. I bet he'd make a good preacher, not some long-winded bozo, like in the Whitehouse.

"You're back," replied the lodge clerk.

"Have a good trip?"

"No, not really. We had a plane accident and we just got picked up today." "You're kidding," replied the young man.

"I wish I wasn't," I said, as I pulled out my wallet.

"I read about you guys in the paper, but I didn't make the connection."

"I hope you have a room?" My energy level was running on empty. I was in no mood for small talk.

"Sure do. A queen bed ok?"

"That's fine."

I gave Gail the room key, and with the rifle on my shoulder, I carried the back pack down the hallway. "I can get some coins and put our clothes in the washer while you take a shower." "Good idea," said Gail.

Gail piled the clothes by the bathroom door. I wrapped a towel around my waist and took the clothes to the laundry room; back in the room I flopped under the blanket and was asleep in two minutes.

"Your turn," said Gail.

"The clothes will be done in ten minutes," I said, looking at my watch through sleepy eyes.

"How was the shower?"

"Wonderful."

"Right on," I said, as I stepped into the bathroom. Fifteen minutes later, with my nose barely above water, I pulled the plug and dried off. I felt fresh, clean and tired…more like a limp noodle, to be more accurate.

Maybe the best therapy for us will be time and sharing our experience with family and friends, I thought. "Babe, will you promise to talk to me if you are feeling like you can't shake the trauma of the trip?"

"I think I will be fine…Like you said, I may have a flashback once in a while…I'll let you know if something lingers," said Gail. That was a nice question, thought Gail.

"Thank you for the concern," said Gail.

I'm hungry, I thought. My stomach was telling me it was time for a hearty meal. I patted my gut and thought, ten pounds less.

"The clothes will be dry in about fifteen more minutes," said Gail.

"Are you getting hungry?" I asked.

"Yes."

"Me too. That hot bath really helps relax the muscles. How's your knee?" "It hurts," said Gail.

"I'll get some Aleve from the pack."

"Thank you. I'm going to see the doctor when we get back, and ask for the shots he recommended," said Gail.

"Have you thought about a knee replacement?" I asked.

"Yes, but I'm not ready to go there yet," said Gail emphatically.

I reflected about the events of the past few days, as I walked down the hallway towards the laundry room. I shook my head in thought as I clutched the bed spread; That gold is going to help soothe my aches and pains for a long time.

Funny, Gail thought, four days in the woods has really improved my appreciation for simple things like clean clothes and showers and food.

When I stepped back in the room I noticed Gail's glowing smile and complemented her about her pretty, rosy cheeks and sparkling eyes. I took her hand and gave her a kiss on the lips. She matched my desire to capture an intimate moment of pleasure. Our kiss led to an embrace. The seconds shared in each others arms tantalized our cup of contentment.

Wearing our fresh clean clothes, we walked past the young male clerk, on our way to the cafe.

"Hi folks…Are you going to be able to recover your plane?" asked the clerk.

"I don't think so," I answered.

"Sorry…Oh, I saw your big bowie knife. My Dad had one like that," said the clerk. I looked at the kid and thought, I better not even go there.

After we were seated in a booth, I mentioned to Gail. "Did you hear the kid asking about my big knife?" Gail nodded her head.

"We've got to be careful that we don't let our secret out of the bag; if we talk about the cabin I'm afraid it will tickle someone's curiosity, and it might come back and haunt us. Word up here goes full circle in a hurry," I said, in a quiet voice.

The waitress took our order; two juicy hamburgers. "I don't think I've appreciated a hot cooked meal more than now," said Gail.

"Hanging around me will do that to ya," I said, with a smile.

Gail said, "No, I don't think so."

"Really?"

"Yes really."

"I'm going to check with the clerk and see if I can get a box for the rifle; it will be safer in the bus cargo area. I was thinking maybe we need to write a "Need to Do List" and prioritize it. I have a ton of things to do in the next few weeks." Gail looked at me and nodded her head in agreement.

"My cell phone should be charged up in another hour.. You want to call your kids?" I said, as we feasted on our delicious dinner.

"Ok, after supper."

Gail looked at the cell phone…five bars, ok, she thought, as she picked up the phone, laid her head back on the pillow, and dialed her daughter's number.

"Hello." Brian, Gail's son-in-law, answered.

"This is your Mom."

"Mom! What a relief knowing you guys are ok," said Brian.

"Sorry for all the drama and stress."

"Hey, it sounded like you guys had a much tougher time. Did Bill have insurance on the plane?" asked Brian.

"Yes."

"How bad was the damage?"

"The wings and wheels were torn off," said Gail.

"That must have been scary," said Brian. "Like the German immigrant says, 'I not can tell you!'" said Gail. "Is Joni there?"

"Yes."

"Put on your speaker phone and I'll talk to both of you," said Gail.

"Hi Mom," said Joni.

"Hi babe. We've showered and had supper and this bed feels sooo good. I thought my camping days were over….let me tell you…. this camping trip was like a trip to Hell. We crashed into the forest. There was no clear place to land. I really thought I was going to die. The trees ripped off the wings of the plane. For a few minutes I thought Bill was dead. I've never felt so alone in my life. Bill was knocked unconscious." Joni's heart swelled with hurt for the pain her Mom was feeling. "I was able to wake him up and we climbed out of the plane. We got our survival gear and moved about a hundred yards out of the trees next to a meadow. The mosquitos were really bad in the wooded area. We discovered grizzly bear sign and Bill felt it would be wise to move away from the meadow; later in the day we went back to the plane to get some water and discovered a bear had ripped up the seats and tore up most of the bottles. My suit cases had been ripped into and my clothes were scattered all over. Bill decided to build a tree platform for sleeping on. I thought it was a lot of extra work; later we found out the tree platform idea probably saved our lives. There was plenty of room for both of us, about twenty feet up in the trees; about 7:30 we went up on the platform and by 8:00 o'clock I was asleep; around 9:00 o'clock a grizzly bear came into our camp and Bill couldn't scare it away. I screamed, like you can't imagine, as Bill fought to keep the bear on the ground. It was determined to eat us for dinner. Bill told me to climb further up the tree, and he shot the bear with his bow. It took several shots before the bear gave up and left. The bear ran off and died during the night. It only got about a hundred yards before it stopped and bled to death. There was a lot more that happened and I will share it with you when I get home."

"Wow! Life in Anchorage is going to be dull after what you've gone through," said Joni.

"You would have been proud if you had seen your Mom climb up and down the tree. Twenty feet is a long way up in a tree," Gail said, triumphfully.

"When do you think you might get home?" asked Joni.

Gail replied, "Two days, I think. We are going to catch a bus and it will be an all day trip."

"You guys made it in the newspaper. Don't be surprised if the press comes around after you get back," said Joni. "I'm going to need a big hug when I get home. Thinking about seeing you all again helped keep up my spirits these past few days," said Gail.

"Mom, you better be prepared for a lot of hugs…there's going to be a long line. We all are looking forward to a minute by minute report from you and Bill," replied Joni.

"Tell Bailey I miss her and that I have a surprise for her.…Oh, would you call the boys?" asked Gail.

"Ok Mom. Keep us informed. Love you."

"I love you too sweetheart, bye," said Gail.

"I'm tired of telling the story but I need to do this," I said, as I dialed the first of three telephone calls..

"I understand," said Gail, with a smile.

Sonnet answered the phone. "Hi Sonnet," I said, trying to sound cheerful. "Did you get the news from Myndi?" "Lilly called me. You must have an angel on your shoulder."

"You're probably right. Sorry for the past three days of stress." "You're both ok.…that's all that matters." said Sonnet. "Hi Myndi," I said.

"Dad!" shouted Myndi.

"Do you remember the bears on our hiking trip?"

"Of course."

"Well, Gail and I ran into a different breed of bear. We were the intended dinner, not a loaf of bread or potato chips. We were attacked and I had to kill a thousand pound angry grizzly. I'll show you a four inch bear claw someday."

"Cool," said Myndi. "I told my students what happened. You ought to write a book about this trip," said Myndi. "I might. You've only heard half the story. What happened the second day of the trip you won't believe….I'll explain more clearly later."

"Is Gail handling all of this ok?" asked Myndi.

"She's fine now," I answered. "She freaked out when she thought I was dead and then she freaked out when the bear growled and charged us. I was very worried, because at one point she collapsed in my arms in tears….both of us experienced a few horrific minutes…first the crash and then the bear attack; that bear was determined to kill us." "Write that book. I'll read it to all of my students."

"Sorry we put you guys through all of this drama."

"Ahh, a little drama helps us all keep things in perspective," said Myndi "Ready for the summer break?" I asked. "Oh yeah!"

"I learned one thing from this trip; I'll never trust a bear again and I'll always pack a big gun out in the woods. I killed the bear with my compound bow," I said, still astounded that I had actually killed such a large animal. "It took four shots to run it off. The big fella ran about a hundred yards and laid down and died during the night. I followed the blood trail the next day."

"That sounds awfully scary. Did you give Gail a big hug after the bear ran away?"

I welcomed the opportunity to answer Myndi's question…"Of course; I'm doing very well in that department….lots of hugs. I better let you go. We hope to be back in Anchorage in a day or two. You take care. Love you."

"Love you too," said Myndi.

Gail was asleep when I got off the phone. I reached over and turned out the light. I didn't go to sleep for some time. Kids, the crash; the bear attack; the nights upon the platform; losing the plane; Hal Wilcox and his reverence for God; the gold and the unfortunate prospector; Gail, and our blossoming friendship. What are you trying to tell me God? A mixed bag of events are going on here…I'm having trouble grasping all that is happening….Like being swept away in an avalanche. You've blessed me by allowing me to find a person who simply wants to share her life and love, no strings attached….you got us on the ground safely and sheltered us from a ferocious beast; you surrounded us with a bunch of men who are committed to Jesus…are you trying to tell me something? Like maybe I need to get back to the subject of life…Like what's it going to be, me living for me, or me living for You? I think You've used Hal to show me something that's lacking in my life…I know my focus has not been what it should…I remember at one time that I walked with You daily and even tried to walk in Your steps. Years ago You lead me to the book 'In His Steps'; For a long time I asked myself the question, 'What would Jesus do? I can't remember for sure, but I think I evolved into a kinder, more loving person for having made the decision to seek to do Your will in my daily life…You helped me recall a song I loved to sing many years ago, called 'In His Time'.

"…..In your time, in your time,
You make all things beautiful in your time.
Lord my life to you I bring,
May each song I have to sing
Be to you a lovely thing
In your time."

You won't leave me alone, will You God? I know once a person has been anointed, by Your saving grace of Jesus, that they can never again be comfortable by sitting on the fence. You know me…I learned as a youngster that You don't play favorites with any of us…You are not going to cut me any slack….If You can use me in Your service, then help me to be Your voice. May my words and deeds be a lovely thing.

"Bill! Bill! Help!" cried out Gail, in her sleep. Gail's nightmare instantly caused me to reach out and hug her. Wet tears fell onto my cheek; Gail grabbed me, like a frightened child clinging to Momma.

"It's going to be ok," I said, as I stroked her curly brown hair. I closed my eyes, and likewise had a flashback, recalling the ugly teeth and loud roar of the bear as it bore down on us, with those dark red, small eyes; a few minutes later Gail went limp and her breathing pattern reflected a restful sleep. This won't be the last of the nightmares, I guessed.

DAY 5, WHITEHORSE LODGE, DAWN

My bladder caused me to glance at my watch…6:15. The light was coming through the motel blinds. I gingerly limped into the bathroom. The hike left my ankle extremely tender. The cold water felt good on my face and eyes. I took two Aleve. Gail groaned from back pain as she sat up in bed.

"Good morning," said Gail.

"Good morning. I have the usual aches and pains, how about you?"

"My back and knee is sore but I'll walk it out in a few minutes." replied Gail.

"Mind if I go get some coffee and read the paper. I'll wait and have breakfast when you come out." I asked. "Ok. I'll be there in a little while."

Scotty McBride, I thought, as I read the name plate on the young male clerks counter.

"Good morning," said the waitress.

"Good morning. I just want some coffee for now. Would you have a paper lying around?" I asked.

"Sure do. Scotty said you had a plane accident."

I nodded my head.

"Where is home?" asked the waitress.

"Anchorage."

"You walked away from it…that's good right?"

"Yep…just a bump in the road" I said… plus a big bump on the head…any more questions lady? I thought. Going back to that place was not what I needed at the moment; it was too raw a topic so early in the morning.

"Hey Sunshine," I said, as Gail sat down in the booth.

"Look at this," I said, handing the front page of the newspaper to Gail. The article I pointed to said that three Washington D.C. Congressman had been abducted and that a suspect was in custody.

"That sounds interesting," I said.

Gail skimmed through the article and said, "It must have just happened. They don't know where the congressmen are," answered Gail.

"I wonder what nationality the suspect is?" I asked.

"Why are you curious about the nationality?" asked Gail.

"Well, it could be a home-grown terrorist not an Al Quaeda affiliate. I wouldn't be surprised if it was a retired US military person who fought in one of the Arab wars…maybe even a Vietnam veteran. There are a lot of disgruntled, unhappy Americans who are fed up with the partisan politics, especially the Libya tragedy that occurred last year. We were left with more questions than answers regarding that incident. No one in the Whitehouse gave a time line of the events as they unfolded. We were never told specifically why no drones or jet fighters were scrambled to help repel the attackers; no one lost their job, and the attackers were never tracked down and put behind bars. All of this occurred while a President was trying to get re-elected. The President's party never asked hard questions or demanded the facts and neither did the liberal mainstream press. It's scary to think that our elected officials and the press would suppress the truth to get someone reelected. Political lies and cover-ups can make a lot of people angry…anyway, I bet the Whitehouse is really scrambling to prevent the press from getting all of the facts as they unfold."

"It sounds like you've had enough coffee for today," said Gail, as she though, Boy, that headline hit a sensitive nerve.

"Huh, sorry, being a Social Studies teacher for thirty years has trained me to go ballistic once in a while," I said, with a smile.

During the course of breakfast, Gail brought up the agenda for the day.

"Will we have time to get a gift for my grand-daughter?"

"Sure. Before we go into Whitehorse, I need to walk over and file an accident report with the aviation people....maybe thirty minutes."

"Mind if I stay here? My knee is still pretty tender," said Gail.

"Sure. We'll be on our feet a lot in Whitehorse."

When I returned to the lodge I called for a cab. We left for town a few minutes later and I had the backpack of gold on my shoulders.

"We need to go to the Whitehorse Police station," I said, to the cab driver. Looking around at the blue sky and green fresh cut grass and the people driving by made me feel so grateful to be back in a world where goods and services were available and life was a whole lot more secure.

The police officer that greeted me was a young man, who spoke in a friendly and professional manner.

"Sir, what can I do for you today?"

"I want to file an accident report."

"Ok. Is this an automobile?" The officer sat in front of his computer and started hitting the keyboard to retrieve the correct form.

"No, airplane." I replied.

"Ok. I need to see your drivers license? I'll also need to see your pilots license and aircraft registration." The clerk typed the information onto the form and I visually scoped out the wall photos and maps in the clerk's office.

"Now tell me the date of the incident."

"June 5, 2012."

"Location?"

"Williston Lake, north end, wilderness."

"Describe what happened."

"My plane engine died; cause unknown. I crashed into the forest. The plane was demolished. There was no fire; no one was injured. The Yukon Civil Air Patrol found us and transported us to Whitehorse. The man in charge of the rescue was Hal Wilcox."

"Would you like to include the Aviation report along with this report?" I asked.

"Yes sir, that would be a good idea. Let me make a copy of the aviation report...be right back.....I will need your signature as soon as I print this information." The officer handed me the report and said,

"Sign right there please." "Did you see any planes or poachers walking about in that neck of the woods?" asked the officer. I was kind of set back by the officer's question, and I hesitated before I answered.

"Yes, well, no to the poachers, or planes, but I do have information about a body we accidentally found." Gail raised her eyebrows at the end of my last comment.

"Excuse me for a minute," said the officer as he walked in to another room. An older fella came out of the room and signaled for Gail and I to step into his office. After introductions we were asked to sit down.

The gentleman pulled out a tape recorder and said, "You folks were flying and had a plane accident and you discovered a human body and you just returned from the crash site; is that correct?"

"That's correct." I said. The officer explained that he wanted to have me write a report about the body incident, giving dates, location and what we observed, including our names, addresses and phone numbers. The officer apologized for the inconvenience, but he said the serious nature of the situation required our assistance. We were detained for nearly an hour. The officer read my report and nodded his head.

"You folks have endured a pretty tough week. Did you crash on a gravel strip or in the trees?" "In the trees; Hal Wilcox headed up the rescue unit. Do you know him?' I asked.

"Yes. Good man. He provides a delicious moose roast every year at the Rotary Banquet.....Did you do anything with the remains?"

"We left it where we found it…about thirty feet from the cabin."

"It sounds like a grizzly nailed him," said the officer. "We will get a field officer on this right away. If that boot is still there we can do a DNA analysis and if we get a missing person report we can follow up on it. That area is very remote…We have your contact information. I appreciate your help. I'm sorry for your loss."

I shrugged my shoulders and said, "It could have been a lot worse… we're both grateful to be alive." "Amen to that," said the rotund gentleman.

As we stepped out into the bright sunshine holding hands, walking down the steps, I said, "I'm glad that's over.….Now, shall we find out where the mining claims office is?"

"Good afternoon," I said, as we stepped into the mining claims office. "Could you help me find a geographical location? Someone asked me to check if a mining claim has been filed for a certain creek."

"Sure," said the clerk. "Tell me the location."

"I've forgotten the name of the creek, but it's located on the northwest shore of Williston Lake, near the second airstrip."

"I should be able to find that," said the clerk. After flipping through two books of topographical maps the clerk narrowed the search down to the northern tip of Williston Lake.

"That is region 4 of Williston Lake: now I need to go to the book of mining claims."

A few minutes later the clerk said, "There are no claims filed in that area." I asked a few more questions regarding the procedure and cost for filing a claim, and then I took Gail's hand and said, "OK, that's all I needed to know, thank you." Zippity do da, what a wonderful day, I thought. As we walked out of the building I said to Gail, "There's no claim on that creek; it's up for grabs, if a person wants to pay a filing fee."

"You're saying someone was getting the gold without a permit?" asked Gail.

"Yes."

"No record, no name...does that mean we have as much right to the gold as anyone?" asked Gail.

"Yes. I doubt if Americans can file a claim. William can," I said.

THE RETURN HOME

I looked across the street at a travel agency office and asked Gail, "Shall we go ask where the bus station is located?" Gail nodded her head.

The bus station was two blocks away. The morning sky had a few small puffy, white clouds and the winds were calm.

"We need two adult tickets for Anchorage, for tomorrow," I replied.

"We have a 6:00 AM departure or a 4:00 PM departure," replied the clerk. "The 6:00 will be good. When does that bus arrive in Anchorage?"

"9:30 PM," replied the clerk.

I shifted the twenty pound load on my shoulders, as we walked out of the bus terminal.

"Shopping time."

"Which direction?" asked Gail.

"I remember there were some clothing and gift shops on that road leading down to the big paddle-wheel boat. If we go towards the river we will run into that road."

"Ok. Those pain pills helped," said Gail.

"I don't know what to buy for Bailey," said Gail.

"How about a stuffed animal?"

"I was kind of leaning that way," said Gail.

I bought some trail mix, and a book of Sudokus. Gail got Bailey a soft, stuffed bear cub, plus a few clothes and a cross-word puzzle book.

"I could go for a light lunch and a nap."

"Ok. You pick the place," I said.

The lunch and cab ride back to the lodge left one more thing to do; call and give the bad news to the insurance company. After the call was completed, all that remained was a leisure afternoon and evening before the long ride home.

There was plenty of time for reflection during the rest of the day. It felt good to rest on the soft, clean pillows back at the lodge. Both of us pulled back to the events of the past four days. Gail went to sleep quickly. I felt restless and decided to head towards the front of the lodge for some fresh air.

"How's your day going Scotty?" I asked, as I walked by Scotty's desk.

"Ok, kind of slow. What are you folks going to do?"

"Catch the bus to Anchorage tomorrow. I might be back this way in a month or so. I plan to come back and salvage some of the airplane equipment." Scotty just listened and didn't offer a comment.

"I was curious….you mentioned you said I reminded you of your father…is he still alive?"

"No, well, I don't know. He left a few months ago, soon after they released him from the correctional facility. He said he wanted to go check out a place where there might be some gold. No one has heard of him since."

Gold….I could talk about that subject too, I thought.

"Sorry….is your Mom around?"

"No, I live with my Grandmother."

"How long have you worked here?"

"Almost a year."

"Is this job working out?"

"It's alright. My Dad said I should go to college and be a teacher or a policeman. I'd like to be a commercial pilot."

"Money a problem?"

"Yes. Grandma has nothing and Dad was in prison and he hasn't helped much."

Tough situation, I thought. Wouldn't it be a bizarre coincidence if it was his father at the cabin? "Have you been up in a small plane?"

"Yes… several times. The school sports teams travel by plane to get to the different schools in this area."

"I can relate to that….as a coach, our teams traveled by plane in bush Alaska." Scotty listened and allowed me to carry the conversation.

"When I come back this way maybe I could give you a flying lesson." "That would be fun," said Scotty, as his face showed a bit of excitement.

"Well, I think I'll go out on the deck and get some fresh air. I hope you receive some good news about your father."

I walked out onto the deck of the lodge and sat in one of the wooden rockers over looking the broad valley, that included the airport, Yukon River and the mountain range beyond. Everyone has a story, I thought, as I reflected about Scotty trying to survive and take care of his Grandmother. I relaxed in the rocker and closed my eyes. Thank you Father for this day. One day at a time; God, I give you the credit for strength, stamina, and direction. The trip didn't evolve the way we planned, but we got more than we ever could of imagined. We're financially blessed. I have no words to describe the peace and joy I feel. Love has blossomed in our relationship…..Thank you Lord…..I don't mind throttling back my gypsy urge to go running all over the country. I understand her desire to slow down and stay away from the RV tripping…..like driving down the Alaska-Canadian Highway…. She has no interest in trying to change me….Go flying….go fishing or hunting…just take your cell phone and let me know you are ok….I appreciate that attitude…I appreciate the way she lets me live my life, such as reading the sports section in the newspaper or kidding me about going on a Republican rampage….she prides herself in voting who she thinks is the best political candidate….well, I do too…usually it's a Republican….that's not my fault. We help balance each other…I'm impulsive and spontaneous and she likes that. She's a good organizer and I'm disorganized half of the time. I'm a physical stay-in shape kind of guy and she tends to be a couch potato; I nag her about her lifestyle and she tries to get a little more serious about a regular exercise routine…I believe we both are a good match for each other, for whatever time we have left in this world. I don't think she has a selfish bone in her body.

I got up after a while and walked back down the hallway to our room. Gail was curled in a fetal position facing me. She opened her eyes and smiled. I sat down and took off my shoes and rolled over and put my arm around her waist and looked into her eyes and said, "I love you." We kissed and held each other tightly.

"Our trip didn't turn out the way we planned. Did it?" I said.

"Not exactly …. I'm not disappointed I've spent the last four days with you." Gail looked straight into my eyes and said, "In the last four days, I've discovered a man that is tender, brave, and someone I think I could enjoy spending the rest of my life with."

"Thank you." I hugged Gail and gave her a kiss on the forehead.

Gail was working on a cross-word puzzle when I awoke from the nap. I glanced at my watch and said, "It's nearly dinner time."

"There are two good movies we could watch after dinner," said Gail.

"What are they?"

'Sleepless In Seattle' or 'The Unforgiven.' Gail won the toss; 'Sleepless In Seattle'.

"Let's go have something to eat," I said.

Dinner was delicious and much appreciated. The cafe was packed to the gills with young college age men and a few women. I thought the patrons were an athletic team, but after asking the young man in the next booth, it turned out they were parachute firefighters that had come up from all over the US and Canada to fight fires in the Yukon Territory. I eyed the group and saw myself in my college days; athletic, well conditioned, out-doorsy, cocky and confident, so full of life.

"They had to pass a rigorous test of stamina and endurance in order to get hired." I said, envying the boundless energy that filled up all of the cafe booths.

Gail sipped her coke and said, "We are all on the same trail. They are behind us a few bends. I've often looked at senior citizens, when I was younger, and wondered if I would get wiser with the years. I can look at these young people and say yes; there is so much these youngsters have not experienced," replied Gail.

"They are behind us alright. I would say a lot of bends and many peaks and valleys," I chuckled.

Both of us had seen the movie, 'Sleepless In Seattle', but we enjoyed seeing it again; at the conclusion of the movie, when Meg and Tom walked over to ride the elevator down the Empire State Building, I said, "That's you and me tomorrow; getting on the bus to begin the first day of the rest of our lives…only God knows what lies down that pathway."

"Amen, hopefully no more plane wrecks," said a smiling Gail.

Gail got her pajamas on and curled up next to me. It felt so good to put my arms around her body and to draw her up close. I pressed my lips on her lips and we seemed to melt together in a blissful sweet embrace. Gail's tender, warm body, next to mine felt so comforting, but it did not remove entirely the painful memories of the past few days. I thought to myself how the trauma of the past few days reminded me of the nightmares and the restless nights trying to get to sleep after I returned from Vietnam. They will probably never go away, I thought.

"Goodnight," I whispered to Gail.

The five o'clock cab ride to the bus station was quiet. There was no traffic until we got to the bus terminal. There were half a dozen people sitting and standing next to the bus terminal wall. I checked in the box; tickets were exchanged and the big burly clerk glanced over at the clock and said, "The bus will be here for boarding in ten more minutes. The coffee shop across the street has donuts and rolls."

"Care for anything?" I asked.

"Maybe a glazed donut and a cup of milk." said Gail.

I turned towards the door and said, "Let's go," as I placed my hand on Gail's waist to guide her to the door. I really would like to wrap her in my arms and give her a big kiss….Am I starting to get like those cowboys, I thought.

THE LONG BUS RIDE TO ANCHORAGE BEGINS

The bus pulled up beside the building. The driver stepped out and said, "Everyone going to Anchorage bring your carry-on baggage and board at this time. If you're going into Alaska you will need to have you passport and documents."

I put the back pack between my feet and we both tested the seats for comfort. A few minutes later the driver collected everyone's ticket and announced that the bus had a bathroom and he reminded us again that we would be required to show different forms of ID, such as a photo drivers license, birth certificate and a passport when we went through the customs in Northway.

"If you have any fruit or plants that are not acceptable the agents may confiscate them…if you have a pet you must have shot records and if you have children you must have birth certificates for each child," replied the bus driver.

Oh my, I thought; I hope the customs agent doesn't go through my back pack. I was stressed all the way to Northway. Upon arrival at Northway, the customs agent stepped onto the bus and checked everyone's ID and asked if anyone had any fruit, plants, exotic creatures or pets. We both shook our heads and the agent never gave us a second look.

"Whew," I said, as I looked at Gail and squeezed her knee. When the agent stepped off the bus I whispered to Gail, "I was afraid he was going to look inside our carry-on baggage."

The next five hours was a blur. When the cab dropped us off at the Remington Arms, we were exhausted and butt sore.

"I'm going to take two aspirin and hit the sack," said Gail.

"See you at 7:45 in the dining room."

I gave Gail a kiss and a hug and headed down the hall to my room. The next morning I rolled out of bed at the usual time, 6:00 o'clock. I opened the box and began to put the survival gear into the closet. I picked up the rifle, and for the first time I looked it over closely and wondered if I could get rid of the rust with some kind of oil; I came to the wooden stock and noticed a name burned into the wood; Mcbride….Oh my Gosh…. did this belong to Scotty's Dad?

WHITEHORSE CORRECTIONAL FACILITY

The Whitehorse sally port correctional officer said, "Let me see your paper work guys." The inmates handed their release papers to the officer. After a few minutes the officer handed the inmates their papers and said, "You're good to go. Who's going on the bus?" One inmate stuck up his hand. "Someone here to pick you two up?" The other two men, who appeared to be Indian, nodded their heads. "I'll take you two up to the visitors center and I'll take you to the bus station."

Jake Keyes, the inmate catching the bus, had friends in Watson Lake, which was about an hour drive by car. There was no conversation during the short drive to the bus station in down town Whitehorse.

The inmate was about six feet four, lean and muscular. His attitude was very hard core and the officer figured he would be into booze and drugs within the next twelve hours. His rap sheet included 10 felonies over the past fifteen years.

When the officer pulled up to the bus curb he reminded Jake Keyes to check in with his P.O. and then he wished him good luck. The inmate gave the officer a cold, 'screw you' type hostile stare and said, "Yeah, yeah," as he stepped out of the vehicle. The officer figured the guy would be back in jail in a month or less.

Jake was told by the Correctional Hearing Committee that if he violated his probation again he would be going to the big Federal Prison, and it would be a lot longer than the two year sentence he had just served.

Jake had already made the choice to violate his parole conditions, if he didn't get his way in the next few weeks. Jake had made up his mind to find his ex-celly. The two had learned about a possible secret gold site and their plan was to go check it out together when they got out of jail.

Scotty McBride, Jake's celly, had a four month head start and Jake figured he was already at the gold site. Jake soon realized, after his celly paroled, that his gold map was missing. Only one person could have stolen the map. Jake's goal had been to get out and get even.

Jake knew McBride had relatives in Whitehorse, so he found a phone book and dialed the only McBride listed; an older woman answered the phone.

"Hello."

"Is Scott there?"

"No, who is this?"

"I'm an old friend of Scott's."

"We haven't seen or heard from him for a long time."

"Well, would you know how I might find him?"

"I have no idea." The lady thought, I wouldn't tell you if I did. "Good bye." "Bitch!" said Jake, after he hung up the phone.

Jake scratched his balding scalp and shook his head. He thought he had better cool down and think this through… one mistake and he would be going back to the slammer.

Jake decided to locate the McBride house and just observe who comes and goes. There was no car in the driveway. Jake figured he could locate the gold site but he needed cash to get there. Jake figured the old woman had a stash of cash hidden somewhere. I could rob her. I would need a mask, thought Jake.

Jake watched the house, getting more anxious by the minute. A young man drove into the driveway and went into the house. I bet that's McBride's boy. He has a son, and the kid looks like his old man. Humm, thought Jake. I could be tough on the both of them or I could act concerned and be honest and tell them I might know where McBride is and volunteer to help find him. I'll be a nice guy, introduce myself and volunteer to help find McBride….They pay for the charter to the gold sight.

Jake stood up and strolled towards the house. He felt he had a good, safe plan that would accomplish his mission.

I hope they cooperate, thought Jake, as he knocked on the door.

"Hello. Are you Scott McBride's son?"

Scotty looked at Jake and hesitantly said, "Yes." Scotty's first thought was this guy had bad news about his father. "You don't know me, but I was your father's cell mate over in the correctional prison. I talked to a lady here earlier today and she said your Dad's where abouts is unknown. Is that correct?" "Yes," said Scotty.

Jake looked at the young man and said, "Could I come in and discuss an idea with you?"

"What idea did you have in mind?" asked a tentative, cautious Scotty. 'Your father might need our help or even worse, he could be injured."

Scotty wasn't comfortable with letting this stranger come in the house but he did want to know about his father, so he said, "Come on in."

Jake met Scotty's Grandmother, who was sitting in a rocker in front of the TV. After they were all seated in the living room Jake said, "Scott and I supplied cigarettes to an old native inmate and he shared with us the location of a gold site. We were going to try and find the gold but I didn't get paroled when Scott did. Your Dad might be at the gold site.....He might need help.

Scotty stared at Jake, and even though his Dad had not been a very stable father, there was still a strong bond, and Jake's proposal had a strong appeal for the younger McBride.

Jake said, "I don't have the money to charter a plane to the gold site and I was hoping you might be able to help me with this matter." Scotty looked at his Grandmother and she knew what Scotty was thinking.

"What would it cost to charter a plane?" Mrs. McBride asked.

Jake said, "A couple hundred bucks." Jake forced himself to mask his excitement as he thought that maybe his soft approach was going to work.

Scotty and Mrs. McBride stared at each other and a few seconds later Mrs. McBride said to Scotty, "You could request a leave of absence. Your boss can spare you for a few days." Scotty nodded his head.

Mrs. McBride turned towards Jake and said, "How soon do you want to leave?" "The sooner the better."

"Scotty, I have some savings and if you want to do this you have my blessings." Scotty took a deep breath and nodded his head.

Jake was surprised this family was willing to sacrifice their savings for a very disappointing man. Jake's youth consisted mostly of seeing his selfish mother and father beat up each other and abuse drugs and alcohol. He was surprised to see a family willing to sacrifice and help out one of their own black sheep.

The two men packed food and sleeping bags and fishing gear; they thumbed their way to Watson Lake.

Bill and Gail had been back in Anchorage less than a month when Bill, with his new plane, took off to recover plane parts. Scotty and Jake left for the gold site a few days ahead of Bill.

Jake showed the charter pilot where they wanted to go and the pilot said, "No problem…I take hunters in there for deer and bear hunting."

The flight took about sixty minutes. There was no conversation during the trip. The pilot, with his head set, was tuned into music. Jake's body language was obvious; he wasn't a small talk, friendly type passenger.

"There's the lake," the pilot announced. "The second airstrip is about ten minutes away."

Jake nodded his head as he acknowledged the pilots remark. The pilot headed into the wind over the lake and touched down on the fine gravel strip with a smooth one-hopper. The runway was empty but there were obvious plane tracks that indicated the strip had been used recently.

"A couple crashed their plane a short distance from here about a month ago. Those tracks are probably from the rescue crew that came in and picked them up…..Do you need a pick-up?" asked the pilot.

"No. We plan on fishing our way back," replied Jake.

"Ok. Did you let someone know where you are and where you will be traveling and when you expect to return?" The pilot sensed that these two men were not very survival savvy and probably were underestimating the challenge of wilderness travel.

"Oh yeah, we let people know," said Jake.

The pilot shook Jake's hand and said, "Have a good one."

As the pilot leveled off he thought that something besides fishing was going on; they didn't have the right gear for a long camping and hiking trip.

"We've got to find the creek and follow it up stream until we come to the cabin," said Jake.

Both men had light back packs. The idea was to follow the shore for a mile or so and to reach a creek coming into the lake. Most likely the creek was south because they never saw a creek as they approached the strip. About thirty minutes into the hike they found what they were looking for; the stream was running high and fast from the snow run-off.

"Cross your fingers." Jake headed inland, parallel with the creek. Game trails paralleled the creek. Trees, pushed over by the winter snow, made the hike slow and tedious. One hour later the cabin was a welcome site for the out-of shape hikers.

"This must be the cabin," said Jake.

Scotty went over to the cabin and yelled, "Anybody Home?" There was no answer. The men noticed there was no cabin door, and like Bill, they figured the entrance was probably a hole in the ground. It didn't take long to find the hole. Once inside, nothing was found to explain the purpose for the cabin. There were no mining tools…just food and bedding. The area around the cabin did not reveal any clues. The stream did not appear to be mined and there were no animal traps that might indicate a trapper occupied the cabin.

"Dam, it looks like the old man lied," said Jake.

Like a tense alcoholic, Jake's demeanor reflected no patience and a foul mood. "Nothing here kid. We were scammed. Ready for a long hike?" asked Jake. Scotty wasn't ready to tackle Jake's question. The disappointment of failing to find his Dad, and being stranded so far from home and being alone with someone he didn't trust all added up to a frozen mind set; like a frozen computer, Scotty needed to reboot to function. A long hike with Jake didn't seem like a wise choice.

"I'm going north. Are you going with me?" asked Jake.

"I think I'll go south." Scotty figured he could fish going south and also maybe he might come across someone with a fishing boat.

"Have it your way." Jake went inside the cabin and took some of the canned goods.

"Well, I guess I'll be moving on," said Jake, as he looked at Scotty.

"Sure you don't want to go with me?"

"Scotty looked at Jake and shook his head.

"Ok. Watch out for the bears and wolves," said Jake.

The big man was barely out of sight when the sobering thought of being alone hit Scotty…like a staggering sucker punch to the head. In thirty minutes the mood of both men had gone from the anticipation of finding someone and gold, to total disappointment. Scotty walked in a circle with his hands on his head. He took a deep breath and shook his head.

I can't stay here very long, thought Scotty. The owner of this place may come back any minute.

With Jake out of the picture Scotty understood he alone was the one who needed to make the wise decisions if he was ever going to get back home. He thought Jake made a poor choice by going north. The mountains were going to be tough and there was little chance of coming across someone who might be able to help him.

Panic and fear were knocking at the door. Scotty thought of his Grandma and how she read her Bible everyday, reminding him from time to time to try and see God all around him…in nature and people. She said God promised to never leave us or forsake us. Grandma, I hope you're right. Scotty was ready to try it Grandma's way.

God if you are listening, I pray that you will help me tonight and help me get back home safely.

Scotty's fear dissipated after a few moments of prayer. Sleep came quickly to his tired, stressed body.

THE REMINGTON ARMS, ANCHORAGE, ALASKA

Life at the Remington was a normal quiet pace. Everyone wanted to hear what happened to us. Folks were asking for a week, WHAT HAPPENED? One of the men in the Writers Club, ninety-nine year old Jim, wrote an article about us and submitted it to the Anchorage Times newspaper. We were front page news in the gossip column while we were missing and when we walked in, unannounced, we were greeted with a lot of hugs and questions.

The ambulance averaged coming by about every other day. Someone either fell, had a stroke or got dehydrated, sometimes so severely they had to be admitted into the hospital. Senior living has its serious moments. Children worry that their parents can't manage themselves safely. The decision is made by the kids to put the folks in a retirement home, or an assisted-living place. Understandably, the new environment, leaving home and moving into a communal setting is a big change and change is not always pleasant…having the car taken away is always upsetting; losing one's independence hurts. Like everyone else, we had our share of aches and pains. We were both concerned about our weight gain, all the while we enjoyed going out to dinner and going to a movie once a week.

Gail researched the topic of Gold Buyers on the internet and found out there were two types of buyers; those who buy jewelry and dentures and those who deal in volume. The buyers who dealt in volume offered better prices. We both agreed selling our gold a few ounces at a time might be the best way to go; there was less chance of attracting attention; leaving the family out of the affair also sounded wise. If a family member needed financial help the resources were available. Wisdom and prudence seemed to be saying, the less people know, the better.

A month after returning from the accident I was ready to go pick up plane parts. I purchased a new/used plane. Gail made me promise to be careful. She knew I wasn't the nimble athlete I was twenty years earlier, and that one fall in the woods could cost me my life.

The return trip wasn't the same without Gail. I missed her company. I missed her a lot. The plan was to fly to the second airstrip in one day. There was about 20 hours of daylight and this would allow time to fly and hike to the wreckage. I called Gail before I descended towards the lake.

"Hi babe. How are you doing?" I asked.

"Fine, kind of boring with you gone. How's the trip going?"

"Good. Good weather and that was a good lunch you made me. I'm about ten minutes from the gravel strip." "Are you okay?" Gail asked.

"You mean like am I fearful of crashing into the forest again?" "Something like that," answered Gail.

"I'm fine. Not perfectly fine…It's like returning to an intersection where I had an accident and instead of looking once I need to look three times to feel safe."

"Are you going to hike to the crash site today?"

"Yes. I have plenty of daylight. I miss you."

"I miss you too. Don't cry when you see that wrecked plane again," said Gail. "Just think of me, thinking of you, as you carry those heavy parts back to your plane."

"Ok…. I see the second airstrip now, so I better pause this talk until probably tomorrow evening from Whitehorse. I love you."

"I love you…be careful," said Gail.

"Ok, later alligator. God Bless."

"Amen, bye."

When I spotted the second airstrip I decided to pass over the cabin and wreckage site. I received a surprise when I spotted the cabin…there was a man waving his arms. I thought, Oh boy, is the guy signaling for help? I circled around and buzzed the man a second time and sure enough it looked like the man needed help. I decided to drop a note asking the man to take his shirt off and wave it if he needed help.

I dropped the cup along with the note. As I passed over the fourth time the man was waving his shirt. Who could he be? I can't believe it. Now I'm the rescuer, I thought.

Seeing the wreckage site again made me think, She was right…it's not a pretty sight. It felt good to be on the ground again. I felt a slight acid reflux burn in my upper throat, and my knees felt a little shaky as my feet hit the ground. Seeing the wreckage again was like slowly opening the door to thoughts I did not want to re-live. No, I'm not going there, I thought. I shook my head, thinking to myself, This too shall pass, as I pulled out the tools and wagon. I strapped on my pawn shop 57 magnum revolver and sleeping bag and headed towards the trailhead that led to the wreckage.

The hike to the plane took about two hours. It was exhausting going up hill and dragging the cart over and around obstacles. I Thought, It's going to be a lot worse with a load of parts. After a short rest and drink, I left the wreckage and headed down into the canyon. Why didn't I bring someone to help me, I thought. I had flash-backs of Gail and I walking the trail towards the cabin. I could, in an unexplainable way, almost feel her presence with me as I descended the well worn game trail.

As I got close to the cabin I was thinking, I better explain that I had no knowledge of the cabins existence. "Hey," I said, as I slowly approached the man's backside. The man whirled around and said, "Mr. Parker?" "Yes. Scotty!"

"Did you fly over me and drop the note?"

"Yes. My plane is on top of the ridge…my wrecked plane." Scotty looked at me thinking, Grandma you're going to enjoy hearing this story.

"What's going on here?" I asked.

Scotty took a deep breath and then proceeded to tell me what had transpired the past few days.

"A few days ago, a man who knew my father in prison, came to my house and told me he was looking for my Dad. I told him I had no idea where Dad was, and then he said he thought he might be able to find him. He said he had no money and that he thought Dad was at this cabin. My Grandma gave me the money to fly here. We didn't find anyone and we didn't find any gold. The man took off yesterday hiking north towards the Alcan Highway. I told him I wanted to stay for a few more days and then maybe go south."

"It's a long rugged hike no matter which way you go. You were actually planning on hiking back home?" Scotty nodded his head. "I could use your help carrying plane parts and then you can ride back to Whitehorse with me."

I'd be crazy to refuse that offer," said Scotty.

"Ok. Get your gear and let's go."

Scotty went into the hole and popped back out with his back pack.

Was it his Dad that was killed by the bear? I thought. I looked around at the small creek and thought of the boot, which was no longer in sight, and the memories sent a sober chill down my spine. Neither one of the men know anything about gold prospecting, I thought.

"Did the cabin appear to be occupied lately?" I asked.

"Yes. There was food and blankets."

"Huh. It might have been a trapper's cabin," I said. I turned and headed up the trail. I decided to take the route where the gold was buried. The tree and rock were easy to spot. The ground cover was undisturbed. That's good, I thought.

"This is working out well for both of us…one less trip for me hauling parts and you will get back home today," I said. When we reached the camp site I pointed out the platform which still had the canvas covered archery equipment.

"Follow me. I'll show you the big fella that attacked us while we were up on the platform."

The bear carcass was still intact. The hide concealed the arrows that I wanted to extract. "There are three arrows in that body cavity, but I'm not going to try and get them now. The maggots will still be feeding off this thing for another six months," I said.

"Let's get out of here." The decaying carcass put out a wretched odor.

"Why did you use a bow to kill the bear?" asked Scotty, as we walked towards the wreckage.

"I had a 22 rifle and the bow. I figured the sharp arrows would be more effective than the piddly 22 bullets. Are you packing a gun?" I asked.

"No. Neither one of us brought a gun."

"People in the wilderness need to have something for protection. That bear would have probably killed us if we had been in a tent on the ground. I don't know if it was crippled and hungry or if it was conditioned to be a man killer. Predator bears are rare, but they do exist."

We paused at the tree platform and retrieved the equipment that was left behind when we were first rescued. The memories, as I climbed up onto the platform, were a mixed bag of emotions; the part of being with Gail was pleasant, but reliving the attack was something that I hoped would someday escape my memory. The crash site, from ground level, brought back a flood of memories; I was able to suppress the thoughts by quickly focusing on the recovery project. The brain can only focus on one thought at a time, so the busier we got with the nuts and bolts the farther I was removed from reliving the unpleasant past.

"If you will remove these eight bolts and take off the propeller I'll work on the avionics." "Ok," said Scotty. The avionics alone nearly filled the cart.

"The insurance company agreed to pay me 50% for whatever I can get for these parts."

Scotty carried the propeller and I pulled the heavy laden cart. The biggest challenge was crossing the creek. The water level had dropped a few feet from where it was a month earlier. Slowly and carefully we crossed over the boulders without any mishap. The trip to the air strip took nearly three hours.

"This job would have been a back breaker without your help," I said. "We should be able to get the engine on the next hike, and with a little bit of luck we will probably get back to Whitehorse this evening." Scotty nodded his head and thought, that'll be nice.

I'll be ready for a hot bath tonight, I thought.

"It was a miracle you and your friend survived that crash," said Scotty.

"You believe in miracles?" I asked.

"Yeah, I guess so."

"Me flying you home is a miracle, I think."

Scotty thought about the prayer he had prayed shortly after Jake left him alone. I prayed for a miracle, thought Scotty. If I mention that to Grandma she'll probably give me a whole sermon on the topic.

"Grandma will be very happy to see me, that's for sure. She will probably say a plane ride home was a miracle." The second trip was painfully exhausting for me. Twenty years earlier it would of just been a good workout; being out of shape and over-weight and having a bad leg was asking for a heart attack.

The plane could not hold all of the parts, so we covered the smaller parts under a canvas in the trees by the edge of the airstrip.

After about a thirty minute rest it was a chore trying to get the cramped muscles to loosen up.

Up in the air I called Gail and told her I would be back at Whitehorse in a short time and that I would call her after I ate and took a hot bath.

"How's this for a lesson I promised you?"

Scotty smiled and said, "I'm very thankful. Your timing could not have been better." "You want to call your Grandma?" I handed the phone to Scotty.

The kid took a big chance to try and find his father....I sensed the young man had a soft caring spirit.

After Scotty finished talking to his Grandma I asked him, "Is your Grandma a Christian?"

"Oh yeah. We don't go to church but she reads her Bible and prays every day. Her favorite radio station is gospel music and one sermon after another."

"I bet she's been busy praying for your safety the past few days." Scotty took a swallow and nodded his head. "The man that came with you has a long way to go. Look at all of those mountains he has to get over...up and down. There are poachers in the area below. The fish and game told me last month that the poachers were taking bears and selling the hides."

Looking at the rough terrain, I thought, How is that guy going to make it without a gun?

JAKE KEYE'S JOURNEY NORTH

Jake looked up at the plane as it flew overhead; little did he know fate would have him sitting in that same plane in a few days.

"Hey! Don't move! I'll blow you in half if you move." A dirty, bearded, burly man was pointing his shot gun at Jake.

"Whoa," said Jake. "I'm just passing through."

"Like hell you are," said the man. "You need to get down on the ground....Face down!" Growled the man. "Put your hands behind your back." The man pulled out a rope and tied Jake's hands. "Follow that trail in front of you." Jake was thinking the dude was in no mood to reason. Do what he says....an opportunity might present itself... must be ready....sure could use that gun, thought Jake.

The poachers were a depraved lot. There was a wretched smell that filled the air around the camp site. Animal skins were staked out all around the camp. The animal fat on the hides attracted the flies and bees. The men were greasy from head to toe. The campfire smoke and the rancid fat from the animal skins saturated the clothes of the hunters.

The men quietly talked among themselves. "Why didn't you shoot him where you found him? He can Identify us. We've got to kill him. You're too soft hearted. He's got to be put down...just like we put down that other jerk that wanted to desert us. Let's hang him from a tree by his feet. We'll figure what to do with him tomorrow."

Jake was strung by his ankles, from a tree limb, with his hands tied behind his back. The rush of blood to his head nearly made him pass out. The rope around his ankles painfully cut into the skin. The men went back to work skinning the fat off the hides.

Jake thought, If I don't get loose tonight I'm a dead man. They aren't going to set me free.

The three men left the camp. Jake used this opportunity to try and loosen the ropes around his wrists. The men returned about an hour later with a massive bear hide. The hide probably weighed two hundred pounds. The men used a ten foot pole to carry the load. Jake pretended to be asleep. The skinny one of the bunch slapped Jake on the back.

"Wake up!" Jake flinched and inhaled. The men knew he was still alive.

It seemed like an eternity before the men decided to turn in for the night. Their sleeping bags were side by side under an A-frame tent.

Jake was able to swing around and see the men. He could hear them snore. The ropes were loose and it was only a matter of time before one hand popped out. Jake benefited from his prison weight training. He was able to swing up and grab his ankles; from the ankles he was able to go hand over hand until he reached the rope; from the rope he was able to continue hand over hand until he reached the limb. Bear-hugging the limb allowed Jake to swing his legs over the limb; from this position it was a simple matter of un-tying the rope that bound his legs. After a couple of deep breaths he lowered himself to the ground. Three rifles were lying against a tree. Jake held onto the shotgun and put the other rifles behind a tree. Get the back pack and run, thought Jake. Slowly, Jake backed away from the two men. The snoring continued. Jake grabbed the rifles and walked out of the camp, the way he came in.

If they had awakened it would have been bloody, thought Jake; this way they will get to enjoy another smelly day and I will get to keep heading north. Those raunchy characters were going to probably roast and eat me for dinner....

Jake stopped..... It occurred that he was letting the men off too easy. Jake sat down the rifles and back pack. He made sure the shot gun had a full choke of shells and he headed back to the camp.

It was time to get even for the pain those low-lifers had inflicted on him. The snoring could be heard before he spied the two sleeping men. Jake took the red hot embers from the fire and covered the ends of the sleeping bags. He slipped back into the shadows and watched as the smoke rose from the cotton fabric bags.

"What the Hell!" The burley one jumped out of his bag and the other man followed suit. The men tried stamping out the fire.

"Freeze you bastards!" yelled Jake. The men stopped and saw the shot gun pointing at them.

"Take off all of your clothes and throw them over here…your boots too! Careful, don't give me an excuse to shoot." Jake kicked everything into the fire. "Sit down…on the ground!" The men were as naked as a baby Jay bird and it was so cold their nipples were stiff. The fire erupted from the pile of new fuel. The sleeping bags were still smoldering. Give it a few more minutes, thought Jake.

"If any of you follow me I'll kill you." Jake walked out of the camp as the flames rose five feet high. I feel much better, thought Jake, as he wore a smile all the way back to the rifles and his back pack.

Jake was in no condition to hike all night. The four hours of darkness was beginning to set in. His bloodied ankles suffered a horrible pain. The trail was too rocky to travel safely. They won't be able to follow me until it gets lighter, thought Jake.

Maybe under normal conditions, Jake's logic would have been accurate, but the two poachers were not about to act in a rational manner. They were determined and skillful at what they did best… tracking and killing.

The path Jake took from camp was the direction the men took. Quietly, one careful step at a time, the stalkers pursued Jake. Anger and natural perseverance drove the men closer and closer to their prey. After about an hour into the hike the men spotted a black shape that appeared to be an occupied sleeping bag. Only a few more feet and another successful hunt would be accomplished. No mercy this time, thought the big man.

A tree limb crashed onto the ground. Jake sprung into action. As the men pounded the sleeping bag with their clubs Jake threw off the brush pile, that provided warmth, and he aimed at the dark mass hovering over the sleeping bag. The shot gun roared and the big fella fell. The other man froze and three more quick shots shattered the silence of the dark night. Two bodies lay prostrate on the ground. Both men were wounded, dying or dead. The short distance and the dark masses made easy targets. Jake just aimed at the center of the dark bodies. The twelve gauge bear shot was lethal and the hole where the blast exited the body was about the size of a silver dollar. Kill or be killed. Jake had no choice. He had been in this situation before. He never went out of his way to kill someone, but he never hesitated to defend himself.

Jake stood his ground. About twenty feet separated him from the men. There was no movement and there was no way he was going to go rushing up to find out the extent of the damage. It was safe right where he was. There was only a faint moaning sound coming from one of the men. He'll be dead soon, thought Jake. After a few minutes Jake walked over and kicked each body. There was no reaction. Jake used a stick and probed each man's torso. Both had received fatal shots to the mid-section. Blood was draining quickly from the bodies.

The sobering moment caused Jake's chest to rise as the somber reality kicked in. I warned the idiots, thought Jake.

The bodies were dragged off the sleeping bag. Blood was everywhere.

TRIP TO WHITEHORSE WITH PLANE PARTS

Scotty dozed off thirty minutes into the flight.

"Whitehorse tower this is Cessna 30052, five miles east over the highway; request to land on runway 270." "Cessna 30052, traffic is clear, permission granted to land on 270." "This is Cessna 30052, roger, thank you."

Scotty sat up and shook the kinks out of his back and shoulders.

"Beautiful sight."

"Sure is," replied Scotty.

I gave Scotty three twenties as we approached the lodge. "Take this. You earned every penny." "Thank you."

"Sorry you didn't find your Dad. Are you listed in the Whitehorse phone book?" Scotty nodded his head. "My name is in the Anchorage directory and if you ever come my way feel free to come by for a visit.... Don't give up on your dreams. Where there's a will there's a way."

In my lodge room I called Gail. "Hi babe. I'm back at the lodge with a load of parts. How are you?" "I'm playing my games waiting for your call."

"It's going to take a few days to get over the aches and pains. My body aches every time I go out and get some exercise."

"Face it, you're not a kid anymore."

"Accept it?"

"Yep. That's it," said Gail

"That's easier said than done."

"When do you think you will get home?"

"In time for dinner tomorrow."

"Good. We are going out for lobster. Over a dozen residents have signed up to go. I hope you are here. I will enjoy sitting next to you."

"I hope to be there. Do you remember Scotty…the kid that took us to the restaurant?" "Yes."

"He was at the cabin.

"You're kidding," replied Gail.

"I flew over the cabin and a man waved at me. I thought there was a problem, so I flew over again and I could tell the fella needed help. He reminded me of you and me, jumping for joy when the plane flew over. Scotty was at the cabin looking for his father. He didn't find anyone and he was about to hike back home. He helped me carry the plane parts to the airstrip and I flew him home. He is lucky I came along when I did. He didn't even have a gun."

"That's amazing. Why did he go to that remote location?" asked Gail.

"A prison inmate, that knew Scotty's Dad, said he thought he might be able to find Scotty senior. Some guy in the prison gave the men a map of a gold site. The kid and the inmate chartered a plane to the cabin. They didn't find anyone and they both figured there was no gold, so the inmate took off to hike back to Whitehorse. Scotty decided to wait another day before hiking out. Neither one of the men knew anything about gold prospecting." I said.

"He's a lucky kid. Changing the subject; I was given a gift today. We are now the parents of a beautiful, blue male six month old parakeet. It sits on my finger. I can't believe how calm it is. It's already stolen my heart."

"Cool. Have you named it?" I asked.

"Sky."

"That's a good name. I've never had a bird. Have you?"

"No,"

"Does it talk?"

"Yes, well maybe someday. Liz had one and so did Lucy and they said that their birds spoke a few words. I don't remember what the words were."

"Well, I think I'll call it a day. Scotty saved me a lot of work. Keep your cell phone handy." "Ok. I love you."

"I love you…Oh, I've been thinking of you thinking of me all day today."

"That was a sweet thing to say," said Gail, blushing on the other end of the phone.

"I wish you were here now so I could snuggle up next to you."

"I would like to be there too," said Gail.

"I'm glad you are safe and sound there at the lodge," said Gail.

"How's the weather there?

"Clear skies."

"Good. I'll give you a call probably mid-afternoon to let you know about when I should be arriving," I replied.

"I'll keep my cell phone close by," said Gail.

"Love you."

"Love you, too, bye," said Gail.

HOME, AT THE REMINGTON ARMS

The next day the plane ride was smooth and uneventful. Anchorage was a welcome site. The tops of the Chugach Mountains were capped with snow. It was three o'clock when I finished tying down the plane. "Hey. It's me. I'm in the car and I'll be there in about ten minutes."

"Ok." Gail walked over to Sky's cage and said "Hi baby." Sky had learned to step up on her finger in just two days of coaxing.

I stopped and picked up a single red rose on my way home. It warmed my heart to be able to give Gail something I knew she would enjoy. Even a bull in a China shop has a heart, I thought.

"Thank you," said Gail, as I handed the flower to her.

"You have time to take a shower and change clothes."

"I'll see you in a little while. A shower will feel good," I said, thankful for a few extra minutes.

The Remington group was always a barrel of fun when they got on the bus and headed to a restaurant. At the seafood restaurant, Esther, a large woman, was sitting next to Gail, and she asked for the cherry stem from Gail's Mai Tai drink. She said she was going to tie it into a knot with her tongue.

I asked, "Huh?"

"I've heard of that," said Gail. Five minutes later Ester handed the cherry stem to me and it was tied into a perfect knot.

"Esther! That was impressive," I exclaimed.

Young and old, cabin fever gets to everyone. The ladies enjoy dressing up and going out once in a while. Being achy and old is one thing, but fun and humor never goes out of style.

I sold the aircraft parts and half of the profits stayed in my pocket and half went to the insurance company.

Gail and I were nearly inseparable while I was in town.

In the privacy of Gail's apartment, we discussed the issue of gold.

"Tell me what you think of this plan. I could take the gold from where it is now and bury it in the woods next to the airport. We can take small amounts on a needs basis and it will be easy to access. What do you think?"

"That's fine," said Gail. "How much more wreckage do you have left to pick up?"

"Just the wheels, yokes and rudders."

"Would you have room for me?"

"No problem. That would be fun," I said.

"I miss you when you're gone. I don't want to miss out on all of the fun." "Well, if you behave yourself maybe I'll let you come along." "Ha! I'll deflate your tires if you think about leaving me behind."

"I was thinking how it might be fun to visit the town of Dawson City. Have you heard of the place?" I asked. "Jack London lived there didn't he?"

"That's right. He wrote the Book 'Call of The Wild'. The town is on the Yukon River about a two and a half hour plane ride west of Whitehorse. They have B&Bs and a casino and restaurants and museums. I looked it up on the internet."

"We could fly to the airstrip, pick up the parts and come back to the lodge, spend the night and the second day fly the two hour hop over to Dawson City; spend the day and night in a B&B and come home on the third day."

"I would enjoy that," said Gail.

"Would tomorrow be ok?" I asked.

"OK."

Gail got on the computer and in fifteen minutes the reservations were locked in.

WHITEHORSE, SCOTTY'S HOUSE

"Scotty, someone's at the door," replied Scotty's Grandmother.

Scotty was stunned as he looked at his father.

"Hi there, you handsome kid." Scotty senior stepped into the living room and spotted his mother in the recliner.

"Hi Mom," said Scotty Sr. as he walked over and gave his mother a kiss on the cheek.

"Did you break your hand?" asked Mom.

"Sorry….I've been traveling the past month to get back home. I walked and caught rides to get to a remote place and then after I got there I walked mostly to get back here. There were no Post Offices where I went." "I've got to go to work." said Scotty Jr. as he silently walked out the front door.

Scotty Sr. walked over near his mother and sat down.

"I've spent many a night sleeping under the stars these past few months and I've been wrestling with thoughts, like the decisions I've been making, and the stupid things I've done that have put me behind bars and caused you and Scotty a lot of grief. The short of it is, I'm ashamed and mad at myself for being so irresponsible for the past several years…..I know words are cheap and don't mean a thing; well, I intend to become the son you can be proud of and the father that Scotty will learn to respect someday. If washing dishes is the only job I can find then so be it." "Scotty and your cell mate went looking for you last week."

"What cell mate?"

"Jake Keyes."

This name gave Scotty Sr. a chill, as he said, "Where did they go?"

"To some cabin down on Lake Williston. When they didn't find you or any gold they split up. Your cell mate hiked off toward the north and the next day Scotty lucked out and caught a plane ride home."

"I went down to the same place, I think. A man got the jump on me at the cabin and he took my rifle and knife and said to leave or he would kill me.

"Your son was willing to risk his life for you. You've got a long way to go before you can balance the scales," Scotty Sr. nodded his head.

"Go clean up. Your clothes are in the dresser where you left them," said Scotty Sr.'s Mom.

REMINGTON ARMS, ANCHORAGE

Gail and I walked down the hall to go play poker. As we walked by the pool table Gail said, "When my 150 pennies are gone I'm going home."

"Me too. We'll see how it goes."

There was a new resident player who insisted on betting a nickel with every hand. This was high stakes gambling for us regular folks. It was bugging everyone to bet so many pennies all the time.

"I'm not going to let him push my buttons. I'll just fold," I said, as the two of us rounded the corner leading into the card room.

"Oh, did you get reservations at a B&B in Dawson City?" I asked. "Yes. We will be close to the Diamond Gertie's Gambling Hall." "We just need to go pick up the parts and fly over to Dawson City." "Right on," said Gail.

"Don't forget your passport," I said.

The trip Friday, from Anchorage to the gravel strip, was calm, clear and smooth. The panoramic view was stunning. The Northway Customs agent recognized us and we were cleared quickly. I told him we had another load of parts to pick-up.

"Want to see the crash site?" I asked, as we got near the cabin.

"No thank-you," replied Gail.

"The gravel strip looks narrow," commented Gail, as we began a slow straight descent.

"This won't take long. Follow me," I said, after a short bumpy landing. The short walk up the gravel bank into the tree line soon revealed the canvas covered parts. I grabbed an arm load and headed back towards the plane. As I approached the downward sloping gravel I accidentally hooked my right toe on a tree root. I did a forward summersault and landed on my back and butt. Gail saw the entire acrobatic flip and was stunned. I did not move. My eyes were closed and I appeared to be unconscious. Gail dropped to her knees and was frightened beyond words. She noticed my eyes flutter and then open.

"Who are you?" I asked, as I looked at Gail.

I gave Gail a big smile and said, "I'm ok. Just teasing."

"You dirty rat!" yelled Gail, as she hit me in the stomach.

"I can't believe I did that without getting hurt."

"You are about to give me an ulcer," said Gail.

"Whew. Let's get this stuff to the plane and get out of here," I said. Think you Lord, I thought, as I stood up and shook the pine needles off my clothes.

"You aren't giving me a whole lot to feel comfortable about…suppose you had been by yourself and broke your back with that somersault?"

"You make a good point, can't argue that." Gotta eat it….Boy, I couldn't do that again if I tried, I thought.

This relationship may not last long if he does tricks like that very often, thought Gail.

The ride back to Whitehorse was filled with thoughts of relaxing, holding hands, laughing, and a hot meal. The lodge was a welcome site.…nothing fancy, just a blue collar economy accommodation. Gail thought, This place will always be special. This is the first place we spent our first night together in the same bed.

Gail rolled out of bed at 6:00 o'clock. She looked at me and felt a swelling of gratitude for our companionship.

"The bathroom is all yours," said Gail.

Breakfast, turning in a flight plan, and gassing up put the departure time at 9:30; two and a half hours later we arrived at Dawson City.

The distance from Whitehorse to Dawson City, via the Yukon River, is approximately 460 miles. For the past dozen years, every June, the city of Whitehorse hosts the Yukon River Quest. This is a canoe/kayak race, with two short mandatory stops. The racers have been coming from all over the world. The competitors have fine tuned their craft to the extent that they have rigged porta-potties below the seats and they have water lines rigged to allow the paddlers to continue paddling 24/7. The winning time is in the 40-45 hour range. The competitors average about twelve miles per hour, depending on the winds and the speed of the current. A third of the racers usually drop out for various reasons, such as cramps, blisters, torn muscles or swamping the boat in the swirling rapids. We spotted several boats on the serpentine Yukon as we flew a straight course to Dawson City.

The airstrip at Dawson City, located a few miles east of town, was a typical short runway and the airport facilities amounted to only a couple of buildings. The planes, that were lined up next to one large building, were a pretty good indicator that people used this building to book flights.

"I'll taxi and park over by those planes and we can go in and ask for more information." All of the parked planes were high wing commuter planes that carried about ten or twelve passengers.

The building's interior included two rows of back-to-back seats, and a small table with fresh brewed coffee. The ticket counter was at the far end of the room.

"Good day folks," said the lady, as we approached the ticket counter.

"I was wondering if it would be ok to park my plane overnight? I'm on the end of the line where the planes are parked."

"That will be fine. You'll need to sign a liability waiver and pay a ten-dollar parking fee." "Fair enough. Is that the customs building next door?" I asked. "Yes."

I noticed the dress of the employees was typical bush environment attire; totally casual levis, blue collar comfortable clothes. The young male pilots were handling the luggage. Most of the patrons seated were native families. There is one highway connecting the outside world and it's a long dusty drive to the nearest town. Airplane travel is the main mode of transportation for the Yukon Territory residents.

The customs official said to check in with them before leaving. We were told we could call a cab or maybe catch a ride into town with someone over at the terminal.

I was reminded of the many small airport facilities I had visited over the years in bush Alaska. This airport was no exception….you usually had to ask around, or wait around until someone was going your way. In this instance the lady at the ticket counter had to make a lunch run into town and was cordial enough to give us a free ride.

The B&B Gail reserved was originally a brothel back in 1898.

"We were lucky to get an upstairs room with a balcony," said Gail. We had a great view of the Yukon River and the main gravel street of downtown Dawson City.

"Cool," I said, as I steped out on the balcony and viewed the Yukon River and some interesting boats. "My binoculars will be good for checking out all the activity on the river and down on the street."

The paintings and lamps and carpets give the room a nice warm homey look, thought Gail.

"We can bring a few Margaritas up to our room and kick back this evening after we finish playing the tourist routine," said Gail.

"Are you hungry?" I asked.

"Is the Pope Catholic?" said Gail, with a contented smile.

"Let the games begin," I said, as we headed down the stairs.

"Watch where you're walking…we don't need any more somersaults," said Gail.

"Yes ma'am."

There were no shortage of diners.

Hand-in-hand we walked down the board walk. I was looking at the architecture. I noticed how the buildings all looked like the original 1900 vintage. Gail was trying to decide where to eat lunch.

"This whole town was a cow pasture before the gold rush stampede occurred; sand and gravel has made this place a lot more livable. Dawson City and Anchorage both evolved from muskeg ponds and tall grassy meadows."

"Ok Mr. History teacher help me pick a restaurant."

After lunch we went back to our room and collapsed on the bed.

I woke up first. A paddle-wheel boat, cool, I thought, as I picked up my binoculars and scoped out the people and the boat's design. The paddle-wheeler was a small boat with the paddle located in the middle, rather than on the end. The huge Klondike, dry-docked at Whitehorse is massive compared to this, I thought. As I thought about the paddle-wheel era on the Yukon, a name popped into mind...Jack London. Imagine Jack London sitting here now. I read 'Call of The Wild' as a young man and thoroughly loved it. London's imagination would probably be working overtime if he were here now...To get his ideas for the book he must have had a keen sense of observation. It is unimaginable trying to survive the hour by hour, day by day bitter cold winters. Gathering wood to keep warm was a full time job, and eating a balanced diet to avoid scurvy was necessary in order to stay strong and healthy. Jack London must have observed the mushers and their dog teams as they ran up and down the snow covered Yukon River. The betting and drinking and fighting in the saloons, and the women shouting from the hotel windows trying to sell themselves...All of this wild, lusty raw frontier life was the kind of scene the world wanted to see and Jack's books described it so well. I bet he got excited as the bits and pieces of his story came together. Who bankrolled him I wonder? It cost a lot of money to get here.....I'm going to research on the internet and get some answers....Were his parents wealthy? Did he live a long, healthy, happy life?

Gail found me on the balcony. She came up from behind and gave me a kiss on my ear.

"See anything interesting?"

"Besides you?"

"Yes." asked Gail

"No."

"Would you like to go ride that thing or go shopping and hit the museum?" I asked, as I pointed towards the paddle-wheel boat.

"What do you want to do?"

"No, you pick," I said.

"Shopping."

There were several gift shops. I'd like to find something to help remember this place, thought Gail. I shadowed Gail and tried not to get bored.

Ah, I thought, here's my chance to get something for her. I sprang into action like a man on a mission. No longer following Gail, like a lost puppy, I scrutinized all of the jewelry for women. It didn't take long for a bracelet to grab my attention.

'Klondike Gold Rush, Dawson City'. The bracelet identified the place, and the small nuggets, shiny dogs and sled were cute. It was a pricey bracelet, but she was worth it. I picked it up and handed it to the clerk.

"Please hold this. I'll pick it up in a few minutes." The clerk smiled and nodded her head.

The museum was the next building on the block. Maybe they will have a biography of Jack London, I thought, as we slowly walked the isles of the museum talking about items of interest. The photographs brought the era to life. People from all walks of life were on the board walks and boats. The streets were muddy and there were canvas tents everywhere. I spotted a photo of Jack London. Here we go, I thought, as I also spotted the biography I was hoping to find. He died young… forty years; he had kidney problems; he married twice; his parents were not wealthy; He struggled financially all of his life; He was bankrolled by his brother-in-law; He filed a claim in November and mined it for a month until he became ill with scurvy; an all meat diet nearly killed him. The doctor said he needed fruit and vegetables, In the early summer he paid for a ride on a small boat and rode 1500 miles down the Yukon to the Bering Sea, where he rode a sail boat back home.

"Be right back…potty-time." I ducked out the front door of the museum and went into the gift store. I paid for the bracelet. She's going to love this, I thought, as I admired the individual pieces attached to the bracelet.

After finishing the tour, Gail said, "That was interesting…especially the way they harnessed the creek water to separate the sand from the gold. The rocker boxes were helpful but once they found the gold, they built the long sluice boxes to get more in a quicker fashion."

"Exactly….that's what gold fever will do to a person…more, more, more."

The next stop was down the street to Diamond Gertie's Gambling Hall. On the way to the casino, my thoughts zoomed in on the idea of a family placer mine operation.

For ten dollars we could get a claim and lock in the gold sight. We only have to show that we earn $200.00 a year to keep the claim active. Hum…. maybe we could do it? William is a Canadian citizen….gotta check it out.

Diamond Gertie's was a large white wooden structure about the size of a full size gymnasium. Once inside, the typical casino sounds caught our attention. There were the usual card and roulette tables and slot machines. Beverage tables and chairs were set up to accommodate spectators in front of the stage where the can-can girls performed every ninety minutes.

I lost my two twenties after about an hour on the penny machines. Gail's twenty had gone up to $127.00 when I came up behind and saw the score.

"How do you do it? Did you get that from your first twenty?" Gail nodded her head with a big smile "Forty pennies at a time," said Gail. I shook my head.

"When are you going to stop?" Gail really was having fun. Her smile seemed to imply she could do this all night. "If I go down to a hundred I'll cash out. How did you do?"

I pointed my thumb down, indicating skunked. Gail's luck took a dive and thirty minutes later she cashed with a nice profit.

The afternoon was spent on the deck. There was a cool breeze. I enjoyed scoping out the boats on the Yukon. "What do you think about our two families spending some summer vacation time at the gold site? We could carry in a generator and a few large tents; us men could harvest the gold and you women could entertain yourselves or help process the gold, or prepare the food and drinks; We could have a radio and lights and could play cards at night. The money could be divided equally."

"Would your family like it?" asked Gail.

"For a couple of weeks …yeah, I think they would go for it." "How much money are we talking about?" "I don't know."

"Why can't you men go?"

"You sure? You would give up the experience of mining for gold?"

"Explore the issue. It sounds interesting. Maybe we ought to discuss it with the kids," said Gail

"Huh…maybe if just two of us go….kind of a trial run. If we do well, then more of the family might consider getting involved."

Put it to rest, I thought, as I took a sip of a Margarita and scanned the sky at a Bald Eagle riding the air currents.

The afternoon consisted of one more trip to the casino, followed by dinner.

"Close your eyes and stick out your hand," I said, as the two of us sat in the diner. Gail gave me a puzzled look and thought, what are you up to now?

"Surprise, surprise," I said. Gail looked at the bracelet and was floored with surprise.

"It's beautiful. Thank you." Gail sat in silence as she admired the new gift. She looked at me and said, "You've just won my heart and soul."

I smiled and said, "I'll settle for your heart," I said.

As we walked back to our B&B Gail said, "Oh boy, it's been a fun day." "Shall we see if there's a game show on TV or maybe a movie?" I asked.

"I'm going to slip into something comfortable. You want to put on your pajamas?" asked Gail. "Good idea."

Gail snuggled up close to me, smelling like a fresh picked rose….. and the rest of the evening stayed in Dawson City.

"I sure slept well. How about you?" I asked, with a grin.

"Very!" smiled Gail. I could go for more good nights like that, I thought.

The morning breakfast consisted of a choice between hash browns, eggs, ham or bacon or French toast. The coffee and food was far better than what we both expected. The B&B experience turned out to be a very delightful time.

I called for cab service to get out to the plane.

"When do you think we'll get to Anchorage?" asked Gail.

"Probably around 3:00 o'clock."

The customs official asked the usual questions, checked the paper work and said, "Have a good flight."

The dusty gravel road to Tok, Alaska, called 'Top of The world' in the tourist brochures, revealed a few vehicles, trailed by a cloud of dust. The community of Tok was about two hours down the road and we both needed to use the bathroom; following Tok the next stop was Anchorage.

ANCHORAGE

"William, Dad here. How are you guys doing? I asked.

"Fine…going to work every day. Are you and Gail still hanging out together?"

"Oh yeah. She's the sunshine of my life. The reason I called was to discuss an idea and get your opinion. Do you have a few minutes?" I replied.

"Sure, go ahead."

"Well, as you know, Gail and I spent a few days camping in the wilderness. We accidentally discovered a small cabin while we were getting some drinking water. My gold prospecting knowledge came in handy. I discovered a primitive sluice box in a small creek beside a cabin. I'm talking about no-man's land, a huge wilderness area. I tested some of the dirt. The short of the story is that the creek produced about an eighth ounce of gold per pan. By myself, I could extract nearly eight ounces a day. Todays market value for eight ounces would be a minimum of twelve thousand. I checked in Whitehorse and was told there are no active mining claims in the area of the cabin. You, being a Canadian citizen, could file a claim at this particular site. The fee to lock in a claim is only ten dollars.… I could go in and spend a few days and thoroughly test it, but I don't think I should risk going alone."

"You seriously think you could get twelve thousand a day?"

"I washed out nearly an eighth ounce of gold in one pan. I'm not exaggerating. I believe there is enough gold there to put our family on easy street for generations. What I'm telling you may take a while to sink in…but the absolute mind boggling truth is we found a gold bonanza. I am talking about thousands of dollars a day…simply using a sluice box and panning for gold…just like the old forty-niners did at Sutter's Fort in California.

"It's hard to fathom..…You sure no one has a claim on the property? Is it on public land?"

"Gail and I went to the Claims office in Whitehorse and checked it out…No claims are registered in that area, and it is on public land. Claims must be renewed yearly, and claims must show a yearly profit of $200.00 or more, or the government will not issue a renewal permit."

"I need to run this by Stef. How soon would you want to do this?"

"My calendar is wide open….there is one thing I should mention…. this situation must not be discussed with anyone other than your wife. If this discovery got into the papers it would be immediate chaos." "Let me talk about this with Stef and I'll get back …how's that?"

"Ok, that will be fine."

"Did you hike in and pick up the plane parts?"

"Yep, in fact I've settled with the insurance and picked up another plane."

"That was quick. What did you get?

"It's an old Cessna 185 with almost all new avionics. It will carry four adults easily."

"Did you consider getting a super cub?"

"No way. Too loud and besides I would be too tempted to land in places where I would probably kill myself."

"Yeah, that makes sense…well, tell Gail I said hi."

"Give me a call."

"Ok Dad. Talk to you later."

"I just got off the phone with William. I asked him if he had time to come up for a few days to go gold digging." "What did he say?" asked Gail, as she sat down a load of laundered clothes.

"He is going to talk it over with Stephannie.….I told him we found gold in the creek, but I didn't say anything about the buried gold. I don't plan to share this information…maybe in a will.…we'll see." As the day went along, all I could think about was going to the creek to test the soil.

"I'm thinking I should fly to the cabin tomorrow. I want to settle a few things." "Like what?" asked Gail.

"I want to transfer the gold over to the airstrip and also do some serious gold panning. I figure before asking William to take time off from work, I should go first; work the dirt and then I'll know one way or the other. This gold thing is bugging me. I think we found a field of gold so rich it will bless our families for a long time, and I would hate to hesitate and allow someone else to claim it."

Am I losing my mind…is this what they call gold fever? My mind was racing full speed. Talking with William, must have triggered this sense of urgency. I know it is risky to go alone, but delay is risky also, I thought.

After putting together a list of supplies, I went to the store and got the food I would need for three days. The excitement of panning the gold rich soil was welling up in my mind. This could be the last great exciting adventure I will ever get involved in, I thought. I wonder if Amelia Earhart was this excited about taking off on her around the world tour?

As I planned out the trip on paper, Gail was zoomed in on her tablet game. The logs can easily be put back into the creek, I thought.

"How long will you be gone?"

"Three or four days." Gail was fearful, but she reacted in her typical fashion with a silent response.

JAKE KEYE'S JOURNEY BACK HOME

Jake picked up the fishing pole and reeled in the ten pound test line. The trap he set saved his life. The first man bumped the line and this pulled down the log, which broke the silence and triggered the whole scenario.

The blood and smell of death was sending signals in every direction. Every bear for miles around would soon be converging on the site. Jake knew he had to move out of the area. The bloody sleeping bag could not be left behind; He needed it to keep from freezing at night; it had to be washed as soon as possible.

Jake looked into the night sky and found the North Star, which was part of the Big Dipper. He had been going north, but he decided going south might be a safer route; more chances of running into someone who might be able to help him get home.

As Jake traveled south, towards the cabin, every once in a while, he spotted shoe tracks in the soft dirt. Jake figured when he came to the creek he would be close to the cabin. When Jake reached a fast moving creek he followed it down stream until he spotted the cabin. The cabin was a much welcome site. It was going to take several days of rest for his ankles to heal. Several days after Jake arrived at the cabin he heard a plane approaching. Little did he know it was a pilot heading his way.

PRINCE GEORGE, WILLIAM'S HOUSE

William discussed Dad's proposal with Stephannie. Stephannie's response was, "I don't care....just promise me a B&B some weekend."

William smiled and asked, "When does school start?"

"Four more weeks...August 14th."

"I'll check the schedule at work. What's a good excuse for a leave of absence?"

"Tell them you have female problems."

"Should I mention your name?" William smiled.

"Funny, funny," chuckled Stephannie.

TESTING THE CREEK FOR GOLD POTENTIAL

"I love you," I said, as I gave Gail a kiss and headed out the door for another trip to the cabin. I had mixed feelings about the trip. I wasn't going to some unknown site, and I was no stranger to gold panning. The hike was going to wear me out and the panning was going to be a lot of physical work. I felt a sense of responsibility for my family to see if this gold adventure was going to become a reality. I could just walk away now, but there was to much 'Indiana Jones' in my soul to turn away and let someone else reap the booty.

This all started when we innocently took off on the trip to visit the kids in Prince George….It's now evolved into something like winning a multi-million dollar lotto ticket. Life usually gives us a few choices, but a large sum of wealth radically increases the choices one can make every day….If this pans out, our children and grand children will reap from the financial yearly harvest. William can file a claim and we can spend a few weeks for a few summers working the dirt. The challenge will be keeping the lid on what we have. Nothing ventured, nothing gained. Que Sere, Sera, I thought.

After gassing up at Whitehorse, the lodge sounded like a good place to get a hot meal before going to the cabin.

Scotty may be there, I thought, as I walked toward the lodge.

"Hey! How's it going?" I asked Scotty.

"Ok. My Dad is back home." I wasn't sure how to respond to Scotty's comment. I nodded and waited for Scotty to fill in the blanks.

"He actually went to the cabin where we were. A man was there and he threatened to shoot my Dad if he didn't leave immediately. Dad had to give up his rifle and a few other things before he left."

"Is your Dad going to hang around and help you and your Grandma?"

"Yes. He said he was tired of chasing rainbows…so he says. I'll believe it when I see it." "People change for the better… some times." "I hope so.

"I bet your Grandma was happy to see you back home in one piece."

"Yeah and then Dad came home a few days later. He got a job washing dishes. He figures he'll get a better job at some point."

"Yeah, remember, where there's a will, there's a way. I better get my breakfast…I have a long day ahead of me." I shook Scotty's hand and said, "I'll see you later."

As I walked to the plane, I thought, Am I living out an Indiana Jones fantasy? My imagination, as I finished my coffee, was running ninety miles an hour. It was good to find out the bloody foot was not Scotty's Dad. Who was the guy? He ran Scotty Sr. off and took his rifle and knife, but that doesn't tell me where he came from. I know for sure he didn't have a claim on the creek. Mining secretly probably happens a lot.

The remainder of the flight was calm and clear. Gail was on my mind so I dialed her number. "Hey, I miss you… It's been a good day," I said.

"Everyone's fine here. Joni, Bailey and I went out to lunch," said Gail.

"I just had lunch at the lodge. Scotty told me his Dad came home, so I'm wondering who was the victim at the cabin."

"Was that rifle and knife his Dad's?" asked Gail.

"Yes." When Scotty's Dad arrived at the cabin there was a man there who wasn't very friendly. He told Scotty's Dad to leave or he would shoot him.

"Did you say the inmate was hiking back to Watson Lake?"
"Yes", I said.
"You plan to be back in three days?" asked Gail.

"Yes."

"What am I going to do for three long days?" asked Gail.

"I'll miss you too."

"No you won't. Gold will be the only thing on your mind." "Wrong. No more than three days." I replied.

"I love you….and I'll miss you."

"I Love you. Talk to you in a few days."

HIKING TO THE CABIN

The back pack, including a sleeping bag, food and gear and rifle weighed about twenty five pounds. Twenty years earlier this would have been a piece of cake, but today it was a challenge. The hike up the creek included several rest stops. I was determined to go at a comfortable pace.

"Ut oh." I was upset because I spotted a blanket blowing in the wind next to the cabin. I was nearly a hundred yards from the cabin, and there were lots of trees to prevent someone from easily spotting my arrival. I'm here only to pick up plane parts, I thought, in case someone needs to know. I wonder who could it be? I thought, as I walked up to the cabin. What am I getting into now? I thought. The additional complication irked my soul.

There was a man sitting on the ground with his back against the cabin wall…sound asleep. A rifle was against the wall about two feet away from the man.

"Who are you?" I said, as the man nearly jumped out of his pants.

"Who are you?" asked Jake, as his eyes went over to his rifle, which he made no effort to grab. Jake had a nervous tone in his voice. I had the jump on him.

"Don't worry. I'm not here to do any harm. My wrecked plane is up on the hill and I needed some water before I haul some of the parts back to the airstrip."

Jake recalled the charter pilot telling about a crash nearby. "You must be the guy that crashed a plane not to long ago?" "That's me."

"Do you know Scotty McBride?" I asked.

"Sure do."

"Were you here with him?" Jake nodded his head.

"I took him home. I came over for plane parts a few days ago, and when I buzzed the wreckage I spotted Scotty here at the cabin. To make the story short I hiked here to see if he needed help…He told me you had gone north."

"Yeah, well I ran into some problems going that way so I decided going south might be a better idea."

I suddenly remembered Scotty saying neither he or Jake had a gun…so where did Jake get the rifle? This guy is an ex–con. I better be careful, I thought. I wonder what kind of problem he had going north?

"Where's home?" I asked.

"Watson Lake."

"I can take you there. It's about an hour flight."

I'm glad I stayed here, thought Jake.

"I'm glad I stayed here to let my ankle heal up…I took a fall and twisted my ankle pretty bad." I figured the sooner I could get this guy away from the cabin the better. "You plan to take me now?" asked Jake.

"We have plenty of daylight. I wouldn't feel right about leaving a man stranded out here in the wilderness."

"I'm Jake. I never got your name."

"Bill Parker."

I filled my canteen with water and we headed for the plane. Jake's thoughts were about the stroke of luck that unexpectedly came his way. He was not watching where he was putting his feet. He was excited about the prospect of being under a roof where there was a soft bed, food and a hot shower in about two more hours. The mountain slope was covered with a fine layer of gravel and Jake's right foot took off ahead and down he went, onto his butt; he wound up with minor scrapes on his palms.

"Shit…I better pay attention," said Jake, as he picked himself up.

"Are you ok?" I asked.

"Yeah, just got careless…I can't believe my stroke of good luck."

"Scotty's a good kid. I met him there at the lodge," I said. "You probably know I knew his Dad." said Jake.

"Yeah, Scotty said you two met each other in prison."

"That's right," said Jake.

I better not mention that Scotty Sr. is home, I thought.

"The Fish and Game in Whitehorse said there are poachers operating in this area. Did you see any sign of them?"

"No," said Jake, and no one will ever see any sign of them, thought Jake.

The brisk hike took about an hour.

The flight to Watson Lake gave Jake an idea what kind of terrain he would have encountered had he continued north. It was one mountain range after another…up and down all the way.

I wonder why he is doing this? He's not getting anything out of it, thought Jake….Could he be a cop?

The airport at Watson Lake was totally surrounded by a thick forest of mature fir trees. Town was about a ten mile drive that connected with the Alaska Canadian Highway on the outskirts of the quiet community of Watson Lake.

"I'd help to pay for your gas but I don't have any cash."

"Don't matter. I'm just glad you didn't have to cross those rugged mountains by yourself. Call it pay back. I know how it feels to be rescued," I said.

We shook hands and I walked over to use the restroom. Jake headed for the highway.

Whew, glad that's over with, I thought.

The rest of the day included the trip back to the airstrip, tying down the plane and hiking back to the cabin. So many memories already, going and coming in this neck of the woods, I thought.

A hot cooked can of stew was on my mind as I walked into the camp area. I was hungry enough to eat a plate full of steaks. A small one burner stove heated up the stew in about five minutes. The cold stream water, some crackers and the stew was totally satisfying. A nap on the bed in the cabin felt secure and refreshing. I was glad Jake was now totally out of the picture. Thanks to the bear encounter, I was experienced enough to know I could not afford to get careless regarding my surroundings. One guy made that mistake and it cost him his life;

I made it a priority to scope out the area every few seconds. I felt secure sleeping in the cabin.

Putting the logs back in the creek was the first thing that needed to be done. The logs would cause the gold to drop and sink on the up-stream side of each log. I saved my food cans to store the highly concentrated gold/dirt. The last thing I would do before I left was to separate the small amount of black dirt from the gold. This was the most exciting part of gold panning…you actually get to see how much you have accumulated. Hour after hour I shoveled dirt from the stream. The current washed the dirt over the logs and the gold settled deeper into the soil. The latter half of the day was spent panning the dirt. Panning was hard on the back, but seeing the gold in every pan was motivation enough to keep sloshing the dirt out of the pan.

Over the next three days I worked practically non-stop. Knowing my labor was going to pay big dividends was motivation enough to keep me going. The idea was to see what a good days work would produce. Going home and getting back to the comforts of the big city and being with Gail sounded more appealing every hour. The process of getting the gold 98% pure was accomplished on the third day. I still needed to go up the trail to retrieve the buried treasure. When I reached the spot where the gold was buried, I looked all around to see if I was being watched. All that gold in one place must have made me feel a little nervous. The eleven bags felt like a ton in the bottom half of my back pack.

The eighty pound load, going down hill, was a careful one-step at a time process.

Several rest stops and two hours later I picked a place near the plane to bury the gold. There were plenty of pine needles and leaves to cover up the fresh dirt.

All that remained was to fly back to Whitehorse and spend the night at the lodge.

"Hey. I'm on the way to the Whitehorse Lodge. How are you?"

"Fine here. I was hoping you would call today. How did you do?"

"I probably have sixteen ounces. That's about twenty-five thousand. I think William will be convinced to get involved."

"Three days, twenty-five thousand….that's pretty awesome," said Gail.

"Yeah, pretty awesome."

"Are you going to try to come home today?"

"I might...If I take a nap at Whitehorse. I'll let you know in a couple of hours." "Oh, remember last week I found Scotty at the cabin?" "Yeah."

"Well, I found the man who was at the cabin with him...the convict fella was at the cabin when I got there. It's crazy. I'll explain when I get home."

"Ok, sounds good. Be careful; stay longer if you need the rest. I love you." "Love you too."

"Oh, William called the day you took off. He is raring to go."

"Good. When he hears what I brought home he'll really be excited. I'm glad I made the decision to get in and check out the situation. Now I know for sure that we have a super opportunity that will benefit our families for a long time."

"It's a blessing, that's for sure," said Gail.

Gail's son, Billy, a solid six foot two inch outdoors man worked for the Anchorage electric company. I enjoyed his competitive personality. He could put away the beer but I never saw him drunk. Billy was good at repairing small engines and I figured, since he was family, that he would be a good choice as a working partner along with my son. I called him and explained what was going on and he jumped at the opportunity. He had vacation time on the books so a two week 'camping trip' was no problem.

The world turns on its axis every day and life for most is a daily grind, but for our families....our lifestyle was about to improve dramatically.

The three of us men made up a list of equiptment and supplies we would need and I did the shopping. My plane, with two seats removed, handled all of our gear.

Gail, William and I met Billy and his wife Dixie at the airport restaurant at 7:00 AM. Gail and I looked at the interior of the restaurant, and as we sat in the same booth that we occupied on our first trip, our thoughts brought a happy smile to our faces. I squeezed Gail's hand and asked, "Does this place bring back memories?" Gail smiled and nodded her head.

We discussed how long we expected to be gone. Gail and Dixie shook their heads knowing two weeks was going to be a long time to be away from their soul mates. We talked quietly how much gold we anticipated bringing home and this softened the disappointment for the ladies. Billy and William were as pumped as I was about the trip. We drove the short distance to the plane. After some last minute instructions and hugs and kisses I untied the ropes from the wings and removed the blocks from the wheels and checked the moveable parts of the plane.

"Let's do it." I said. William got in the co-pilots seat, Billy behind him and I climbed into the pilots seat. The ladies got into their car and drove over where they could view us taking off. We were facing a beautiful clear day as we lifted off. We spotted caribou as we were about to pass the Talkeetna Mountain area. We had a nice tail wind as we crossed into Canada. The Whitehorse Airport was a good stopping place for lunch. After refueling we took off on the last leg of the trip, only two more hours to go.

William and Billy were blown away when they saw the crash site.

"Wow! Your knees must have been shaking when you came down in those trees," said William shaking his head as he looked at the twisted fuselage and the two separate wings.

"Those wings will make excellent sluice boxes. We can drag them down the mountain to the cabin, and we can use the gasoline for the generator and pumps," I said.

Two trips were required to get the equipment to the cabin. It was an exhausting six hours of back and forth labor transporting the gear and setting up the camp. The following morning we hiked up to the wreckage site.

"Boy Dad...you guys could have easily been killed." The somber reality sunk in as William looked at the wreckage.

"Tell me. It wasn't our time....Let's go up the trail. I want to show you our camp and the bear."

"There she is ...our penthouse," I said, as I pointed up to the tree platform. "William walked over at the base of the tree and looked up. "Pretty cool." "Go up, check it out."

"The bear was only ten feet away when it stood up on its hind feet."

"Pretty hard to miss at that range," said William. I'm sure glad I didn't experience this, thought William.

"This place brings back memories…Gail climbed on up there when the bear attacked," I said, as I pointed towards the tree with my finger.

"Mom climbed up there by herself?" asked Billy.

"She sure did," I said proudly.

William searched his father's eye's as his Dad described the few harrowing moments of the attack.

"The bear slowed down after the fourth shot and slowly walked away into the dark of night. It didn't go far.…Come on, I'll show you the carcass."

"Holy cow!" shouted William, when he saw the partially shrunken carcass. William's respect and appreciation for what his father had accomplished was broadly enhanced after seeing first hand, the bear, the tree platform, and the crash site.

"I'm impressed Dad."

We gradually got the camp set up with a tent, generator, porta-potty, shower and food. The ripped off wings at the wreckage site contained about forty gallons of aviation gas. The gas was drained into eight plastic buckets. The aluminum wings were dragged down to the cabin. Billy used a pair of sheet metal clippers and separated the wings.

There were four pieces that made up the forty-five foot sluice. The makeshift sluice box was a good attempt to filter a lot of dirt. Three high-banker sluice boxes, along with three two and a half horse gas pumps were purchased. These machines were amazing the way they filtered the sand so efficiently. The three high-bankers and some more equipment at home was all that was needed to separate the gold from the fine grains of sand. There was never a dull moment. Two weeks would go fast and speed was important. Sore muscles were doctored via over the counter pain killers. The plan was to filter the dirt twice and take the remaining gold concentrate home where it could be filtered one final time.

WATSON LAKE

Nearly a month had past since Jake's failed attempt to find gold at the cabin. Jake sipped on a beer as he looked out the window of the run down trailer.

Suddenly the thought occurred to him that maybe the pilot who flew him home so quickly had a reason to get him away from the cabin. He seemed to be in a hurry to get me out of there. How did he know about the cabin…it was a long distance from the wreckage. Maybe he discovered gold and didn't want me near the cabin, thought Jake.

The hunch Jake felt about the gold began to grow legs. Jake figured it would be easy to find out if there was a registered mining claim; it would be a public record. The office was in Whitehorse. Jake's intellect and street savy made him a dangerous man if someone crossed his path. I'll check out the claims office tomorrow…If I'm right, then maybe I can put together a plan that will put me on easy street for a while, thought Jake.

Jake was choosing to go down a pathway that had serious consequences, but, in spite of his intellect he was blind to the possibility that he might lose his freedom forever.

"Good morning," said Jake, to the Yukon Territory Whitehorse Mining office employee.

"Good Morning. How may I help you?" asked the employee.

"I'm thinking of filing a claim and I'd like to know what my options are?" said Jake.

"Do you have a certain location in mind?" asked the man behind the desk.

"I was thinking about the area in the upper Williston Lake region," replied Jake.

"Give me a minute to find those charts," said the clerk. "That area is wide open for filing. I see only one claim that's been filed in the past few months" said the clerk.

"Could you show me where that claim is located?" asked Jake. The clerk put his finger right on the creek where the cabin is located.

"Ok. I am thinking about going into that area, so I may be back," said Jake, as he shrugged his shoulders and gave the clerk a smile. I was right…now it's my turn to get a piece of the action, thought Jake.

Jake had no money to get to the gold site, and even if he did there would be a record of him going there and the cops could put him at the location on a specific date. The fact he just visited the mining office could incriminate him if any harm came to Bill Parker. He needed a plan that would have no witnesses. Jake needed to find out the name of the pilot who gave him a ride and he needed to find out where he lived; how to get this information; that was the question. The kid knows his name, thought Jake. No, I've got to stay away from the kid, thought Jake. Maybe Scottie could help me do this job? The guy crashed his plane…maybe the aviation people at the airport have a record? Jake walked into the aviation office and asked the clerk if there was a record of a plane crash about two months earlier in the Williston Lake area. Jake explained that he was looking for work and that maybe the man who crashed the plane might need help salvaging the plane parts. The clerk quickly found the specific information Jake requested, including name, telephone and address. Jake wrote down the information and said, "Thank you."

"Good luck," said the clerk.

Jake figured Bill Parker was probably keeping the gold at his home in Anchorage…that's where Jake would need to go. Jake was broke and he thought he'd check to see if his ex-celly was home.. Resources, like friends and money were scarce. Jake had burned more than a few people in the past by not repaying loans. Why not see if he could pan handle the McBride family. If his ex-celly was home maybe he could help him do this robbery. Jake went to Scotty's house and knocked on the door. Scotty's Mom answered the door. She told Jake that Scotty Sr. would get home around 5:30. Jake nodded his head and left. There was no pleasant conversation, like, "How is your son doing," Jake knew she didn't trust him and he wasn't going to waste time or breath on her. The afternoon went slowly as Jake waited for Scotty Sr. to get home. Scotty pedaled his old Schwinn bike over to the side of the house and turned to face a flushed angry looking man who reflected a long over due grudge in his eyes.

"I take it you didn't find any gold?" asked Jake.

Scotty shook his head.

"Listen man, I came here to see if you would be interested in helping me go after some gold. A man In Anchorage, Alaska is mining the gold we didn't find. I aim to get some of it and I could use your help," said Jake.

"You mean like robbery?" asked Scotty Sr. Jake nodded his head.

Scotty Sr. looked hard at Jake and said, "I'm through chasing rainbows. I'm going straight from now on…my family and freedom is more important than gold."

Jake stared at Scotty Sr. and no more words passed between the two men. Jake turned around and never looked back. Scotty Sr. went into the house and explained what had just transpired between Jake and him.

"Good," said Scotty's Mom, in a tone of voice that seemed to approve of her son's decision to reject Jake's offer.

BACK AT THE CAMP

The operation was going smoothly. The soil was saturated with gold. The gloves we brought were a life saver. It was necessary to use the hands to filter out the larger rocks that accumulated in between the sluice boards. The current was strong enough to flush the sand along the full length of the forty foot sluice box. One person shoveled and the other two agitated the rock and sand to help the gold settle to the bottom. Using gravity and the flow of the stream it was fascinating to see the lighter particles flow over the logs, knowing that the gold was dropping down to the bottom of the box. The first half of each day was spent accumulating gold in the box. The afternoon focus was to further filter the gold through the high-bankers. We placed the hoses in the creek and cranked up the gas operated pumps. Each high-banker had a six foot sluice, and we shoveled the gold concentrate into the sluice box and then watched the sand flow over the slats as the gold wedged up on the bottom. Every few minutes we would wash the sluice box gold into a bucket. Looking for the larger flakes was non-stop excitement. Every few minutes someone would yell, "Got a big one!" We produced approximately forty eight ounces of gold the first full day of work. With ten more days of vacation time left for Billy and William, I figured we would harvest over a million dollars worth of gold. The sheer amount of gold was shocking and sobering to the degree that it was hard to stay focused on the job of filtering the dirt hour after hour. A steady job with this kind of money, drawing interest every month; plus harvesting this amount of gold every summer…it was like having a weird dream where you figure to wake up any second, but yet you are also hoping the experience is real. Each day went fast and the sweat and blisters were visible proof of the challenge of shoveling dirt ten hours a day; the body ached from head to toe.

"I see two problems," Billy said, as we sat at the table eating our dinner inside the tent. "Keeping this place a secret and getting time off from work. There is so much gold here it boggles my mind and my job only allows me to be gone two weeks a year."

"I was thinking along that line myself," I said. "Part of me says I need to stay here and work the gold until it runs out, but that is not realistic or practical…same for you guys. This gold is not going to go away. As long as we renew the claim every year we can come every summer. I can live with a seasonal gold mining operation. People who have fish permits in the Bristol Bay area can only fish in the summer and they make a good chunk of money. A seasonal job is ok with me," I said, looking at William and Billy.

"Part of me says drop everything and make this a six month job, but I agree…family should come first. We are going to walk away with a lot of money. Have you thought about how to split the profits?" asked William, as he looked at his Dad.

William caught Billy and me off guard with the question. "I hadn't thought about it. How about a three way split, and if there are four of us next summer we can split it four ways?"

William and Billy shrugged their shoulders. "Think about it. Sleep on it." I said.

"I wonder why the man you found here didn't file a claim?" asked William.

I shrugged my shoulders. "I guess secrecy was more important. I know there is a sixty-three page packet that has to be filled out and also the government inspectors come around at least twice every summer… some people don't want to be bothered." I said

"It makes me a little nervous knowing a killer grizzly might still be around, plus maybe someone who feels they have a right to the gold." said William.

"Sounds like we are experiencing the same feeling that other gold prospectors felt; like we are, or will be in someone's sights sooner or later." said Billy.

"I think you might be right," I said. "Gold prospecting is a very secretive fraternity and it has it's share of cut throats. When I lived in California I canoed and fished in the Sierra Nevada Mountains, and one day a store owner at the lake told me a grisly story about some Chinese prospectors. During the California gold rush thousands of prospectors panned all over the state. There were thousands of Chinese working on the trans-continental railroad project, and when news broke about the discovery of gold near Sacramento, laborers, Chinese included, slipped away in the middle of the night and rushed to the gold fields.

The Chinese working in the streams beside the white men was not tolerated. Discrimination was alive and raised its ugly head. The white prospectors persecuted, to the point of murder, a lot of Chinese who tried to pan for gold. The Chinese, to their credit, did not run and hide; they just went further into the wilderness in their quest to satisfy the gold fever that consumed all of the prospectors. A group of Chinese found gold on the San Joaquin River, far back in the forest, and they built an elaborate sluice that covered a half mile. Their secret site was discovered by white prospectors and the Chinese were ambushed and murdered. Some of the men were tied to logs and pushed into the river. There was no law to punish the guilty. East coast law and order came to California, but not until a lot of people fell victim to the blood thirsty greed of evil people. The campground where I camped was called China Bar. The big sluice box is still visible," I said.

Sitting in our tent, protected from the mosquitos, munching on dinner, our conversation was revealing something that seemed to have a grip on all of us; we were developing a paranoid feeling that someone was looking over our shoulders; prosperity attracts attention.

"Like winning the lottery…this is getting more complicated by the hour," I said.

"Exactly what I was thinking. I've been thinking about what I'm going to do with a quarter of a million dollars, just from two weeks of work," said Billy.

"I've been thinking about that too. Guess I'll discuss it with the brains in the family and figure out something," said William.

"Billy took a drink and said, "Last year someone broke into our house, while we were gone for the weekend. They got everyone of my guns. I went out and bought a five hundred pound safe."

"You saying I should get one of those?" I asked Billy.

"I learned the hard way…sooner or later everyone gets robbed," said Billy.

We were five days into the operation. The equipment worked perfectly. Right after breakfast William discovered something very alarming. "Check this out!" William was standing over a fresh set of grizzly tracks.

"I wonder if its been coming around every night. If this were Yosemite, California I wouldn't be very alarmed, but this is not California and this is not a pet bear. I think we need to move into the cabin. This thing is going to come back. Bears don't give up easily. You guys have any ideas?" I asked.

William and Billy had no immediate answers.

"This reminds me of our attack while Gail and I were on the platform. I can't believe this is happening again. It reminds me of a shop teacher from Naknek, Alaska who shot a record size grizzly in his chicken pen. The bear wouldn't leave the chickens alone and the man came face to face with the monster in his chicken pen. One shot twenty feet away luckily dropped the bear in its tracks. This guy will visit us every night until we stop him," I said.

"It's a shame we can't scare it away," said William.

"I tried that. It didn't work," I said.

"We could do three hour watches and shoot it tonight if it comes back," I said.

"Get it over tonight; sounds good to me," said William.

"What do you think of this idea? Put out some bait. One of us sleeps on the cabin roof and if the bear shows up we plug him," said Billy.

"I like it. It sounds safe. Three hour watches?" I asked. Billy and William nodded their heads.

After another exhausting day the men leveled the cabin roof just before hitting the sack. That should work, I thought. Lets draw straws who takes the first watch," I said. William got the short stick.

"You're next Dad," said William.

"Ok. Take the binoculars and count the satellites. Is the headlamp good?" I asked.

"Billy tested the headlamp. "Works well," he said, as he shone the beam of light on the tent thirty feet away. William hiked up the log and crawled onto the roof. The sleeping bag did little to soften the rough round log roof. Billy handed up the rifle and William chambered the 180 grain bullet and took off the safety. William figured a silent squeeze of the trigger would do the job.

"See you in a few hours, maybe sooner," I said, as Billy and I headed down the hole and into the cabin. The entrance into the cabin was to small for a bear to crawl into, so we knew we were secure.

"As William settled into his bag his thoughts went home to his wife. 'Be careful,' she would probably say if she knew what I was doing. Dad attracts drama and adventure like bees to honey, thought William. The starry sky was glittering alive with stars and satellites and commercial aircraft. It was a pristine clear sparkling night that one remembers years later. The clear dark sky begged definition. How did it all come into being? William knew his Dad would say, 'God created it all.' Belief, how do you get over that hurdle? Thought William. William pondered the multiple directions he and his wife could go with the money. She is going to be shocked when she finds out we have harvested nearly a quarter of a million a piece, thought William. William peeked at his watch under the cover of his bag. The first two hours had gone fast. An owl nearby was the only sound William had heard since his watch began. The large creek nearby was loud enough to drown out the sound of crickets. He could hear the men snoring inside the cabin.

"William suddenly stiffened when he heard a noise that sounded like it came from the side of the cabin. The log he used to get on top of the cabin roof sounded like it fell onto the ground. William moved slowly as to avoid making any noise. He flipped the switch to turn on the lamp and then with the rifle in both hands he threw off the bag. By leaning towards the edge of the roof he found himself looking at the butt end of a huge brown mass of fur. A bear had it's head in the hole that led into the cabin. Shit! It's trying to go into the cabin, thought William.

"Hey! Whispered William. The bear came up out of the hole and stood up on it's hind legs. William took this clear chest shot and squeezed the trigger. The animal went down without so much as a step in any direction. The blast was incredibly loud. The animal dropped almost immediately. One of the men inside the cabin yelled, "What's up!"

"Stay where you are!" yelled William. The bear didn't move. William put one more bullet into the animal to make sure it was down for good. "Be careful. There's a bear only a few feet from the door. It's dead, I think." yelled William. Billy slowly stuck his head out of the hole and saw the big ball of matted fur, only two feet away.

Shit, thought Billy, as he popped back into the cabin. William held the light on the bear and watched to see if the animal was breathing. A minute or two went by and Billy tossed a stick that struck the animal; there was no movement; the intruder was dead.

Billy and I crawled out of the hole very quickly. William kept the rifle in a ready position in case the bear moved.

"Good timing. I was not looking forward to being up on that roof," I told my son. William cracked a big smile.

"That tent doesn't make me feel secure," I said.

"If you hadn't built that tree platform you and Gail might not be alive today," said William. I nodded my head. Removing the bear from the camp was no easy task. We managed to roll the bear into the fast moving stream. Mother nature and all of her critters would do the rest. Inside the secure walls of the cabin, getting to sleep came slowly.

After a hearty breakfast After a hearty breakfast and discussion of the past nights event we got after it again. The clock was running and everyone was motivated to maximize their time to harvest as much gold as possible. The next three days went smoothly and quickly. More gas was going to be needed soon.

During the afternoon of the seventh day I asked the guys if they wanted to go get gas and groceries and a good steak dinner. They jumped on the proposal. In less than an hour, after we had hidden the gold, we were ready to leave for the plane. We each carried two empty five gallon gas cans.

Up in the air everyone called their spouses and talked briefly, promising to call later in the evening.

"I would suggest you guys not discuss anything about gold on the cell phone. The government monitors all cell phone conversations, and I don't want some IRS agent knocking on my door asking questions," I said. A whistleblower recently leaked that the government had been monitoring all cell phone conversations for years and that congress knew, but was told, for securityreasons, not to reveal the facts to the American public.

The weather had remained clear the whole time since we first began the operation. Whitehorse was a welcome site. It was about 6:00 PM when we tied down the aircraft and began the hike over to the lodge. We planned to check-in and catch a cab and hit the steak house. Scotty was at his check-in desk. It was a happy moment for me seeing the young man who, inspite of his dysfunctional family, was persevering. Like the young lady in the movie 'True Grit', his attitude and character reflected qualities I admired.

"Scotty, how are are ya doing?" I said.

"I'm doing fine. Just can't stay away from this place can you," said Scotty.

"Got a room for three grubby men?" I asked.

I paid the bill and with key in hand started to walk towards the room when Scotty asked me a question.

"Mr. Parker, could I talk to you for a minute?" asked Scotty, with an awkward expression on his face. I handed the key to Billy and stepped over by Scotty's desk.

"What's up?" I said, as I gave the young man a curious look.

"Well, I'm not sure where to begin...My Dad has a job and is trying to live a responsible, law abiding life; that's the good news; the bad news concerns you." Oh boy, where is this going? I thought.

"Really," I said, as I sat down in the chair next to Scotty's desk.

"My Dad mentioned to me two nights ago that he was approached by Jake, his ex-celly. Jake thinks you filed a mining claim at the cabin. He knows where you live in Anchorage and he tried to convince my

Dad into going to your place to rob you. My Dad refused to help him. That's all. I was going to call you."

"Wow! I wonder how he got my address," I paused, trying to absorb Scotty's statement.

"I'm glad you shared this information with me. I never felt comfortable with that guy," I said.

"I felt the same way," said Scotty.

"Could I have your home telephone number? I might need to contact you," I asked.

I wrote down Scotty's telephone number and told him I was glad his father refused the offer and then asked one more question before the discussion ended. "Did your Dad contact his parole officer to discuss this matter?" Scotty shrugged his shoulders to imply he didn't know. I thanked Scotty for the information and walked down the hall as my brain worked hard to figure what to do next. "Oh boy," I whispered to myself…"Police involvement may be necessary. Gail may be in harms way." I decided not to discuss the problem with the guys; no need to ruin their dinner. I wanted to explore my options. As we rode the cab into town my head was in the clouds. Why me? He must be a desperate man. He sounds a little wacko to me, I thought. Anger was kicking in. I didn't appreciate the unsettling prospect of someone robbing me. In spite of the annoying latest challenge, I still savored every bite of the delicious dinner. When we got back to our room I decided it was time to discuss our problem.

"We have a problem….remember I said wealth attracks attention? Well, it's come home to roost. Scotty, the desk clerk, informed me earlier that there is a man plotting to rob me at my home in Anchorage," I said.

I shared the story about Scotty's Dad and his ex-cell mate. I mentioned that Jake supposedly had my name and address and that he tried to recruit Scotty's Dad to travel with him to Anchorage for the purpose of robbing me. I told them that Scotty Sr. refused the offer.

"I think Gail might be in harms way. I don't know how much information this Jake fella has on me. He could be on his way to Anchorage as I speak. Should I involve the police here in Whitehorse? Any ideas," I asked, as I looked at the guys.

"If he knows where you live then you have a problem," said William.

"The cops have to have a reasonable assurance that you are going to be robbed. They probably will not put an officer in your apartment unless you see the guy in your neighborhood...not very comforting," said Billy.

"Maybe I could call the Whitehorse police and tell them the story... maybe they can put some heat on him and explain they have him on their radar," I said.

"That sounds like a good start...you may want to pick up one of those safes like I bought at Cabelas," said Billy.

"Another predator is on the horizon, it sounds like to me," I said.

I walked outside to the front of the lodge and sat down in one of the rustic chairs and dialed Gail's cell number.

"Hi babe," I replied. I jumped right into the situation that weighed heavily on my mind.

"I need you to go to my room and take the backpack that has, you know what in it, and put it in your laundry basket in your apartment, and leave it there until I get home. Tell Gloria she can clean your apartment after you return home." I explained that Jake was planning on breaking into my apartment to rob me. I also explained that I was concerned about her being at the Remington while I was gone. He had information on me and I told her that he might also have information about her.

"I'd like for you to go to Billy's house until I get home. As soon as I hang-up go move the backpack and then don't go near my place until I get home. Billy will explain to Dixie that you're coming over."

Gail was struggling to process the alarming news. Moving out of her place for five days was going to be a pain.

"I would prefer to stay in a motel for five days," said Gail.

"That's fine. I understand. Listen, you need to go as soon as possible. Can you be out of there in the next two hours?" I asked.

"Yes. I will fill a suit case and be out of here before nightfall. I'll take my cell phone," said Gail.

"Good. It will give me a huge peace of mind knowing you are in a safer location. After I get home I'll make a few phone calls and find out if Jake is under surveillance in his home town. I'm going to talk to the Whitehorse police in the morning and see if they can put some fear into him and let him know his plans are well known…maybe this will cause him to re-think his idea," I said.

"There seems to be no end to your life of drama," said Gail.

"I know you love every minute of it," I chuckled. "Myndi would say, 'Go for it Dad; it's good book material.'" "It's going to be a long five days. I worry about you," said Gail.

"Remind me, when I get home, to tell you what happened earlier this week," I said.

"What! You tell me now!" said Gail.

"We had a visitor, more like an unwelcome intruder come into our camp. A grizzly came into out camp and William was waiting for it on top of the cabin and shot it. We haven't had any unwelcome visitors after that incident. We are sleeping in the log cabin. We don't feel secure in the tent," I said.

"I'll call Dixie and get Billy's version of the story, and you wanted us women to go," said Gail.

"Don't mention anything about the contents of the backpack," I said.

We said our 'love you's and called it a night. I whispered a 'Thank you Lord' for my sweet heart friend, as I walked back down the hall to our room.

After breakfast we caught a cab into town and the first stop was the Whitehorse Police station. I talked to a detective and explained our delimma. He said he would contact the man's Parole Officer and suggest he come down hard on the guy. We got our groceries and had the cabbie take us to the plane. After we topped off the tanks and the additional five gallon cans, we loaded up and headed for the cabin.

"Ready to get back and finish the job?" I asked my co-pilot William.

"Yep. That was a refreshing twenty-four break," said William.

The next five days were tedious and slow passing. I couldn't shake worrying about Gail's safety. Everytime a feeling of fear swept over me I gave it to the Lord. On the last day of work we packed everything carefully into the cabin. The fuel was drained from the pumps. The food was left in the cabin. We had four half-filled five gallon buckets of rich gold concentrated black sand. We all had our hands full of items to carry to the plane. The trip was as tough as all of the other previous trips. Everyone was physically drained when we arrived at the gravel airstrip at 7:00 PM. We all were anxious to get up in the air so we could call our loved ones. A week without communication was tough.

"Hello," answered Gail.

"Hello, Beautiful! Everyone's fine here. How about you?" I asked.

"Ok here. I haven't been home so I don't know about that," answered Gail.

"I'm worn out, but knowing you're ok boosts my morale. We hope to be there tomorrow afternoon. Stay where you are until I get there, ok?" I asked.

"Ok," said Gail.

"We are heading to Whitehorse and I'll call you in the morning after we get up in the air. I love you," I said.

"Love you, too," said Gail.

"Billy and William called home and were relieved that everyone was fine and excited about being reunited soon.

"Just think, two months ago Gail and I left home for a few days of R&R and now look how it has evolved," I said.

William shook his head and smiled.

"How long do you think it will take to filter out all of the gold?" asked Billy.

"A few coffee cans every day; maybe a month. Are you guys ok with splitting the gold three ways?" I asked. Both of the guys said it seemed fair.

"Only a lucky few have experienced what we've seen and done. I think we'll be talking around the camp fires for a long time about what's happened this past two weeks," said William.

"I'm glad we got some pictures," I said.

"Thank you for inviting me along," said Billy. I gave Billy a thumbs up sign.

I called the police detective who left me his calling card. I was informed that Jake couldn't be located; his contact person hadn't seen him for nearly two weeks. I didn't want to spend so much time on the phone, up in the air, but the news of Jake's disappearance stirred up a panic attack of concern for Gail.

"Hi Babe. Listen, Jake has disappeared. His P.O. can't find him," I said "You're saying he might be heading this way?" asked Gail.

"That's a possibility," I said. "Watch your back. Did you tell anyone at the Remington where you are staying?" I asked.

"No," said Gail.

"Good," I said. "Stay where you are."

Whitehorse was a welcome sight. The gold/dirt was put into plastic bags and loaded into a backpack. Billy put the pack onto his back and we walked over to the lodge. I felt a little uncomfortable as we approached Scotty's desk. My privacy was tarnished considerably now that Scotty was aware of our gold mining operation. I didn't feel like chatting with the kid at that moment, but I did say I would talk with him later if he was around. I was not handling the news about Jake's disappearance very well. We all washed up and headed for the café.

Jake thumbed a ride heading out west of Whitehorse. He had an address that was burning a hole in his pocket. Help or no help, he was going to Anchorage. Cash was a problem, but he figured an opportunity would present itself out on the highway. There were lots of summer tourists and bicyclists heading for Alaska and camping in the roadside campgrounds. Jake didn't have a passport, but he figured it would be easy to sneak through the woods at night and pop back out on the highway in Alaska. Jake thumbed a ride heading west out of Whitehorse. A broke, homeless man lives from one meal to another. Spotting a vulnerable victim was a refined art for Jake. He detested panhandling but had resorted to it a few times. Robbery was his preference for surviving. Like a savy fox, Jake was good at thievery and his stomach was telling him that he needed to find a meal soon. Hitch-hiking was difficult, even in the Canadian wilderness. Jake figured to steal a good cross-country bicycle from some unsuspecting sleeping biker. The plan was to deflate a tire and thumb a ride from one gas station to another. He figured people would be sympathetic to a biker traveling the AlCAN Highway with a flat tire. The idea worked great. A blanket was all Jake had to keep him warm at night. The ground was hard and the blanket was not thick enough to keep him warm. The sooner he could get to his destination the better.

The weather, the following morning, was clear and calm as we flew over the sleepy city of Whitehorse heading for Anchorage. Gail drove up to the plane as we were chocking the wheels and securing the plane with ropes. Billy's wife also drove up as we were loading the gear into the car. It was a happy reunion. Two weeks was a long time to be separated from your best friend.

William had to catch a plane and Gail and I were anxious to get home, hopefully to an un-disturbed apartment.

We drove into the Remington parking lot and unloaded the dirt. Billy's suggestion about buying a big safe sounded more practical by the minute. Only an idiot would put all that gold in the corner of a closet. The apartment was just the way I had left it. We left quickly to get William over to the big international airport.

Jake's flat tire trick was very effective. He rode into Anchorage in the back of a pick-up truck as the three of us left the parking lot heading towards the airport. The retirement center was only a few blocks from the convenience store where Jake got directions. Jake parked the bicycle by a lamp post and walked into the Remington Arms Manager's office. His arrival was only minutes after Gail and I had left for the airport.

"Excuse me. Could you direct me to 119," asked Jake. The female staff lady pointed down the hallway to the left. Jake walked past a few residents who were napping on a sofa in the main lobby. Jake was hoping to avoid Bill Parker. He didn't want to run into him in the hallway. When Jake got to Parker's apartment he saw the name Bill Parker. He leaned his ear up to the door; there was no sound. A lady across the hallway came out of her room and the two stared at each other for a second.

"Looking for Bill?" asked the lady.

"Yes. I'm an old friend," said Jake.

"He's suppose to be back soon. I think he went fishing," said the lady.

"Thank you," said Jake. Jake left the building quickly. He would comeback when everyone was asleep. An hour later Gail and I arrived back home. We passed Liz, the lady who talked to Jake.

"Welcome back you two." Liz said. We both smiled and before we could utter a word Liz said, "Oh, someone was here looking for you a little while ago."

I felt like I'd just been touched by an electric cattle prod. "How long ago was that," I asked.

"Forty-five minutes maybe," replied Liz.

"What did he look like? I asked.

'A little taller than you; broad shoulders; 40 years old. He smelled like he'd been camping and he had a five day old beard…pretty ragged looking…oh, he also seemed to have a Canadian accent." replied Liz. That last comment was a zinger.

"Ok. He knows where I live," I replied. Liz had no idea what I meant.

Gail and I stepped into my apartment. We left the door open. He might be hiding in here, right now, I thought. We looked under the bed and in the closet. I felt like I was back on the platform again looking face to face at another angry predator.

"What are we going to do?" asked Gail.

"How about if we call Kevin?" I asked. Gail nodded her head. Gail's family included a retired sheriff and a current Anchorage police officer. Kevin, a promising three year career police officer, Gail's grandson, was recently promoted to the motorcycle squad and the swat team.

"Kevin can you talk to your grandma?"

"Sure. What's up?" replied Kevin.

Gail explained the whole story including Jake's visit earlier.

"Let me run this by my boss. I'll call you back in a few minutes," said Kevin.

An hour later my cell phone startled me.

"Hello. I am Kevin's supervisor, Anchorage Police. It sounds like we better stake out your apartment. I can appreciate your concern. I am sending an officer over to your place in the next few minutes, and he will explain how we are going to tackle your problem. Can you meet him down at the front desk in about thirty minutes?" asked the officer.

"Yes sir, I'll be there," I replied. I told Gail the cops were en-route and that they would explain their plans when they arrived. We headed down the hall towards the front desk.

I was expecting to see a black and white drive up, instead a plain-clothed man walked through the swinging front door of the complex.

"Moses!" exclaimed Gail. Moses put his finger to his lips and said, "Let's go to your apartment." The man who was assigned to the stake-out was a semi-retired officer; a close family friend of Gail's. Mose's was a handsome, athletic Hispanic male who walked with an air of confidence. He was retired, but happily volunteered for special assignments, such as a stake-out. We quietly walked to my apartment.

"More than likely this guy will come back when he figures everyone is asleep," explained Moses. Moses looked around the apartment and said, "Let's put some pillows and a blanket on this recliner; make it look like you dozed off watching TV. I'm going to leave the TV on and leave the door unlocked; we'll make it easy and quiet for him to come in. If he comes in I'll arrest him." I thought how bizarre the stake-out reminded me of the two bears.

"Can you stay in Gail's apartment tonight," asked Moses.

"Sure," I said. We all shook hands and Gail and I headed for her apartment.

Jake walked the bicycle, in the dark, to the back of the complex. The outside door was locked but Jake was able to wedge his pocket knife into the door jam and access the building. It was quiet as Jake walked softly down to Parker's room. Jake looked like trailer trash on steroids. He looked like the incredible hulk that smelled like he hadn't taken a bath in six months. Sleeping in the bushes every night and scrounging in the dumpsters for food scraps was not his choice of lifestyle, but he figured the sacrifice would soon pay-off. When he got to Parker's apartment door he leaned his ear to listen for any kind of sound. The TV was on. He slowly turned the door knob. It was unlocked. He slowly opened the door to the point where he could see someone was asleep in the recliner. Jake raised his bat and swung down hard, with all his strength, crushing the person under the blanket. Moses stepped out of the bedroom and yelled, "Police, drop the bat!" Jake was caught in his own ambush. He was out-foxed and should have done what he was told, but he didn't; Jake raised the bat to strike his opponent and Moses fired his revolver, aiming at center mass. Jake went down quickly. Moses called for back-up. Officers swarmed into the parking lot quickly. The apartment alarm was triggered and the manager greeted the officers. An ambulance with the siren blaring followed the police into the parking lot. Someone was being treated by the medics in my apartment, as residents stuck their heads out into the hallway.

"That's my apartment. Is Moses ok?" I asked a young officer standing in the hall. Moses stepped from my room into the hallway and explained that the suspect attacked him and that he had to shoot him. I stepped back from the busy police and medics. The gurney rolled out of my room a few minutes later. Jake's face, even with a grubby beard was recognizable. As I walked back to Gail's room I said to BJ, the manager, "I may need a new carpet," BJ flicked his eyebrows and shook his head. Gail was stunned when I told her that Jake was the culprit.

"Is Moses ok?" asked Gail. I nodded my head and said, "He had to shoot. Jake came after him with a bat." "Gail called her daughter. "Hi, babe. Ready for a shocker?" "I hope you have a good excuse for waking me up," said Joni.

"Someone just tried to break into Bill's apartment. The police used Moses to catch the guy," replied Gail.

"Are you serious! We play cards tomorrow night. I'll get the details from him," said Joni.

"He had to shoot the guy," said Gail.

"Is Moses ok?" asked Joni. Gail explained that Moses was fine and that everyone's nerves were a little frazzled and that we were ok. I went back to my apartment and Moses came over to me.

"Did you recognize the guy?" asked Moses.

"Yes. His name is Jake Keyes, and he came here from Watson Lake, Yukon Territory, Canada. I have the name of a detective who can put you in touch with the guy's parole officer," I said.

"Good," said Moses.

"Can you stay in Gail's apartment tonight?" asked Moses.

I nodded my head.

"Which predator would you prefer, a man or a grizzly?' I asked Moses.

Moses said, "They are equally dangerous. He would have killed you if you had been dozing in the recliner." I rubbed my nose and shook my head in surprise.

Everyone in the Remington, who could still appreciate a sunny day, had questions about the robbery. I simply said it was a robbery and that they caught the bad guy. With the family it was a different story. Everyone was stunned that someone came all the way from Canada to kill and rob me. Jake was extradited back to Canada and was given a fifty year sentence. His spine was partially severed and he was permanently paralyzed from the waist down. I bought a condo situated high near a Chugach Mountain green belt overlooking the city of Anchorage. My gold fever shot off the chart every time I processed a few cans of gold concentrate. The following summer Gail and I punctuated our love by saying our marriage vows. Will the drama ever cease? Probably not.....

ABOUT THE AUTHOR

Robert Hardgrave, a parent, pilot, and retired schoolteacher, followed his dream of publishing a novel. He currently lives in California.

www.ingramcontent.com/pod-product-compliance
Lightning Source LLC
Chambersburg PA
CBHW021442070526
44577CB00002B/248